Online Law Practice Strategies

How to Turn Clicks INTO CLIENTS

Jabez **LeBret**   Mark **Homer**

Online Law Practice Strategies:
How to turn clicks into clients

By Jabez LeBret and Mark Homer

Get Noticed Get Found

7577 Central Parke Blvd Ste. 204

expert@GetNoticedGetFound.com

Phone: 513-444-2016

Fax: 415-520-0332

Earnings Disclaimer: All income examples in this book are just that – examples. They are not intended to represent or guarantee that everyone will achieve the same results. You understand that each individual's success will be determined by his or her desire, dedication, background, effort and motivation to work. There is no guarantee you will duplicate any of the results stated here. You recognize any business endeavor has inherent risk for loss of capital.

Application Disclaimer: The topics discussed in this book and the advice given is specifically for attorneys. Since each state has separate guidelines for both best practice and the ethical ramifications of establishing an online presence you, the attorney, are solely responsible to take the appropriate steps to check with your local bar association and conduct due diligence to verify what advice in this book you can or should take action on. Be responsible – call your bar before you apply these techniques.

Contents

A Special Thank You

Mark and I wanted to take a moment to thank a few leaders from our team for all their help with researching topics, staying educated on the latest and greatest, and diving into our analytics data to separate what works from what doesn't. Thank you for holding down the fort and providing amazing support while we focused our time on this important project. Thank you to Chris Casseday, Haley Biel, Chris Voda, Emily Bush, Megan Thobe and Adam Cassidy.

An extra special thank you to Kelly Ament. Without her eagle eye, sharp wit, and great patience this book would still be getting finished. Mark and I received drafts and updates from her at all hours and through weekends. It goes without saying that she worked extremely long hours but we wanted her to know how instrumental she was in this project.

Thanks to our friends and fellow SEO experts that believe, as we do, sharing information is more valuable to the community at large than hoarding it. Many people contributed interviews to this book, thank you for your time and great wisdom. Also, thank you to PR NewsWire and Fujitsu for offering insights to other aspects of this market and of course, for providing extremely valuable products.

Of course a huge thank you to our family and friends. Working long hours and completing a book tour while revising your book can be a little stressful. Thanks for putting up with us and the many late nights, at times we felt like roommates.

A final thanks to our great clients. Thank you for trusting us with your online reputation, it is wonderful to work with you all.

INTRODUCTION

"**R**eally?" We thought to ourselves. "A book about the Internet?" We shuddered at the thought. The Internet changes every day... and a book, once it's printed, will be around forever.

Still, we realized that while the Internet is almost constantly changing, there exist tried and true principles that will never change. In fact, these principles will only increase in effectiveness as the Internet grows and traditional advertising fades away.

Welcome to round two, version 2.0, the latest and greatest information on properly positioning your firm online. This revision is important because it address several major shifts in the world of properly establishing a web presence, especially for law firms. Things have changed a lot in a year, so grab a pen, and start taking notes (this book should be written in, corners folded, and look like it has been re-written by you before you finish).

This book has the best of both worlds: the stable principles as well as the updates and changes.

What you find inside are the stable principles. In other words, they work... when you implement them. They are based on the rock-solid strategies that we have been using for our clients for years.

The results speak for themselves.

Of course, there will always be elements that change occasionally: when we came across one of those elements, we decided to add an online section of this book for those of you who want the latest and greatest. Look for the big boxes that say "Technology Alert." That will take you to a blog post on our website with the most current data on that particular topic.

One piece of advice: use the resources. They will help you stay on top of the changes that are sure to come. We specifically chose to call out the things we are certain will be changing soon.

On that note, the difference between average practices and *great* practices comes down to implementation. One attorney differs from another often only in their willingness to implement the things they learn.

The same is true for the information in this book. It works, and, similar to everything you learned in law school, it only works when implemented. You *knowing* all of this information won't help you achieve any better results with your practice. When you *implement* it, this information will allow you to help more people, create a more stable firm and gain some bragging rights at the next conference you attend.

Use it... and send us your success story.

Speaking of implementation, one of the most common questions we get from attorneys is, "How am I supposed to get all of this done?"

The answer is that smart attorneys know how to build (or find) good teams.

Let's be really clear and upfront: OUR AGENCY DOES ALL OF THESE THINGS. Toward the end of the book, we have included a section on where and how to find competent people to help you implement your web strategy. That may or may not be our firm. We are as selective about the clients we work with as you are. In full disclosure, we are a digital marketing agency that provides real, positive results for attorneys looking to develop their online presence and their firm. We are obviously going to tell you are about ourselves, but we will save that information for later. The very last section is all about us.

Until then, read this book, take notes and ask yourself a lot of questions about where you want to see your firm in the next 12 months, 18 months or 3 years.

So, let's get started.

"This book is very helpful for helping people with limited understanding about building Internet visibility, to learn how to create and improve their online presence. It has loads of very practical suggestions, written in a style that is thoroughly understandable to those of us who aren't experts."

ADRI Mediators, Memphis, TN 38018

CHAPTER 1

Local Business and the Internet and Your Law Firm

Congratulations! You're already ahead of your competition, just by getting to this first chapter.

Why? Well, most people don't take the necessary action for success. You've gotten this far: now, let's go the rest of the way together. Right now, you might think that, as a local law firm, the Internet may not help you all that much. People know you, you are or have been in the yellow pages, and you're still getting business from referrals.

Who searches for a local lawyer on the Internet, anyway?

The majority of your potential clients, that's who.

Recent research shows that, increasingly, fulfillment of online searches is done overwhelmingly by local businesses. A 2010 study by BIA/Kelsey and the research firm ComStat found that a staggering 97% of consumers research their purchases and local services online before they fulfill them at a local business. This isn't just the case with local services, either: major e-retailers are being beaten out by customers who research products online and then choose to buy them at local stores. This seems to speak to the fact that people like human interaction; they inform themselves online, but in the end, they want that personal connection.

The consequence of this is, unfortunately, any business or firm with no (or substandard) Internet presence is left out of that research process. People want to fulfill their online searches locally, but if you don't pop up when they're doing their research, you'll simply fly under their radar and lose their business to another firm who has that Internet presence.

This is, of course, potentially very dangerous for any local business owner who has thus far avoided being on the Internet (or whose website is not producing results). It may sound alarmist or nonsense, but it's true: the majority of potential clients are looking for a business' representation on the Internet, even preferring it over more traditional media like the yellow pages, radio or TV. In fact, a recent 2009 study by comScore and TMP Directional Marketing showed that, for the first time, the number of clients searching for local businesses on the Internet exceeded that of the yellow pages, and the yellow pages have headed downhill ever since. That was in 2009 – What do you think those numbers look like today? The fact of the matter is that people simply don't use the yellow pages anymore since the Internet is a much easier and more convenient way to get information.

It's surprising at first, but it begins to make sense once you think about it. You can even look to your own habits as proof of this changing trend: how often do you use the yellow pages to find something you're looking for? Do you run over to your desk and flip through the yellow pages to find what you need, or do you do a quick Google search and find what you need immediately? Even if you're still a frequent yellow pages user, take a look at others: your kids, friends and family. How many of them use the yellow pages? If you're honest with yourself, it won't be surprising at all that the way people look for services has changed.

What *is* surprising is how many firms still have huge portions of their budget devoted to the yellow pages and print ads. Many firms can have $20,000 or more allocated to their yellow pages advertising budget, which is, in this day and age, simply a waste of money. Yellow pages just aren't returning enough business to justify that sort of major investment. Of firms that can or do track ROI from print advertising campaigns, virtually all of them have seen diminishing returns. Every month, without fail, more people are using Google and other search engines instead of traditional media and methods of research: this isn't just a passing trend. Search has supplanted the yellow pages, and it's here to stay! An effective online presence isn't just a temporary strategy; it's a far-sighted approach looking toward a future that has search engines as the main tool customers use to make their decisions.

Radio and TV are also seeing large declines in local business advertising effectiveness. Again, looking at your own behavior, have you heard a recent radio advertisement and called that company? What happens more often than not is the average consumer will hear a radio advertisement or see a TV advertisement and immediately go to Google to research that company. If your firm lacks the proper web presence, you run the risk of losing a potential client when they search for you because they will not be able to properly validate the who/what/why of your practice.

When you step back and take a look at the return on the investment, the whole question about where to allocate your resources becomes very clear: the Internet returns better on your investment dollar for dollar than all other major advertising mediums combined. There is still some value in radio and TV, though. We will discuss later how to correctly integrate a TV or radio campaign with a properly established web presence.

WHAT THAT MEANS FOR YOU

So, how do you get in on this corner of the market? Don't big businesses and large law firms dominate search engine rankings on the Internet? Can local businesses and firms even compete in this ferocious online arena?

As it turns out, they can... We will get to that in a moment. The real first question to answer is, "Where are people going?"

If you've paid attention to the news about online behavior, there is no question that people are using social media networks for more and more of their overall Internet usage. However, the fact still remains that Google is the number one search engine. This does not mean that you should only focus on Google and ignore the rest of the Internet. In fact, it is quite the opposite. We will discuss at length the areas you should focus on, how much energy and time you should spend on each and how to use those to build a solid web presence. That will come in later chapters. First, let's turn to Google, the king of search engines, and see why Internet search is a relevant option for attorneys.

Google has, in the past year, made some of the most significant changes to their search algorithm that we've seen in a long time; specifically, they've shifted searches for brick & mortar businesses to something called "local search return" or Google+ Local, a feature that used to be only available on their Google Maps service.

What is a local search return? Originally, when a user searched on Google Maps, local businesses would pop up in the area the user was searching for. If a user searched "Estate Planning Attorney New York, NY," for example, the Google interactive map would appear with helpful markers placed around the map, indicating local businesses nearby that fit the search request. Restaurants and hotels were the first businesses to jump on this feature and utilize it, and it was a natural fit: visitors to a new city need to know places to eat and sleep, and the Google Maps local search return feature was very useful to both users and customers by showing users where these local businesses were and facilitating that offline conversion.

Very soon, however, businesses besides restaurants and hotels realized that this service could benefit them greatly, and they began listing themselves on the local search return maps as well. Eventually, Google realized that if users were searching Maps to get this kind of information, many of them were also likely searching in the regular search box as well (located at Google.com), not realizing that they had to go to the Maps section to get the local search results. Again, look at your own search habits. How often do you go to Google Maps to search for something? Most likely, you simply type it into the Google. com search box and hit enter.

At this earlier point in time, Google's regular search box was just returning lists of links as search results; they weren't map-based and often weren't nearly as useful as the map results that Google Maps was returning.

Now, however, you can apply the information in this book to establish your firm on the map specifically for people in your community so that when they search for your services, you pop up right on the front page of Google.

This is possible because Google started incorporating the local search returns into their regular search page. Thanks to Google's changes, when you search for a brick & mortar business now, it returns a map as well, with up to seven marked locations on the map that are all local businesses. (Which makes sense). If someone is searching "Real Estate Attorney in Denver, CO," they do not want to see results for attorneys in Charlotte, NC. Users want businesses located near where they are. Google also added a feature that automatically determines your location when you enter a search on Google.com. This is great news for local businesses because there is now a real chance for competition: two years ago, local businesses simply couldn't compete on a national level with giants like Amazon or Wikipedia. Today, however, there is a higher likelihood that your firm can show up in the top three results on a local search page, which will boost the amount of prospects calling and emailing your practice on a weekly basis – as long as you set things up properly, which we will discuss at length later.

(FIGURE 1 AND FIGURE 2)

FIGURE 1. GOOGLE NATIONAL RETURN

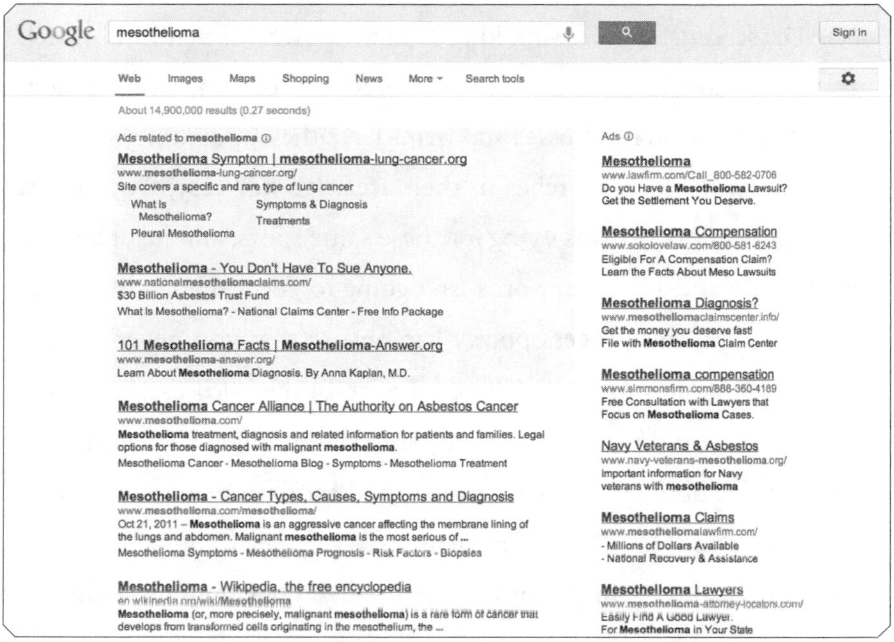

FIGURE 2. GOOGLE LOCAL RETURN

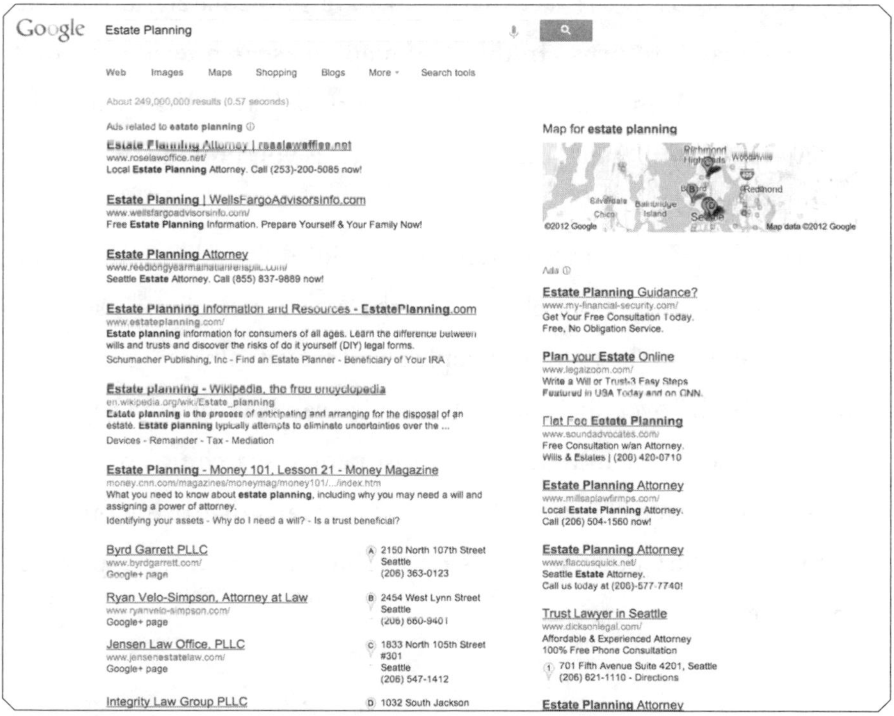

The screenshot here should prove how powerful that local search return feature is. Before, you had no chance of competing in any search; now, local businesses and firms have the opportunity to come out on top for local searches in their area. It's not easy, true. There are plenty of other firms vying for these same spots, and just having a website up and some keywords isn't going to get you anywhere (and in fact, doing this process poorly can ensure that you never see the front page of Google at all). There is an established process, nevertheless, and if you do a good job, are careful and follow all the instructions in this book, you'll have a very good shot at hitting the A, B, or C spots on your local search return!

This is a very important image below, courteous of Hubspot http://www.Hubspot.com. It shows where people's eyes first move when they are given a search return on Google. What is profound about this study is the fact that people are immediately looking at the local search returns. In this heat map, the search term used was "Pizza." Something that, even though very different than your law practice, is a local search just like the services you provide.

(FIGURE 3)

The stats are astounding. Returns for slot A, B and C in the main search area garner more clicks than the entire rest of the page! As you can see from the graphic, people avoid the ads almost completely and skip right over the national organic search returns. They also don't look at the map that often. Most people searching go straight to A without even thinking about it. This means that being on page number one of Google is still essential, but getting to the top three spots is even more crucial.

Figure 3. Hubspot Eye Scan Graphic

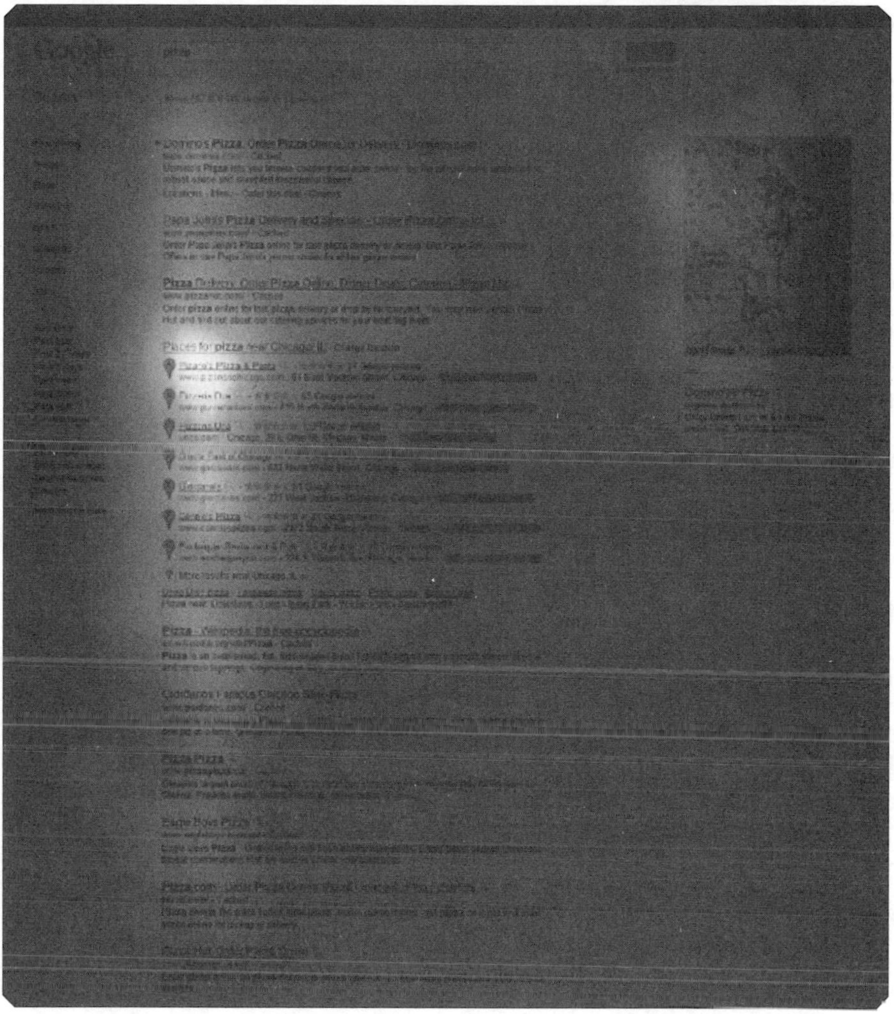

W A R N I N G

DO YOU REMEMBER, just a few paragraphs ago, when I said that this process is difficult? In a similar vein, be very, very wary of companies that tell you that creating a successful online presence is easy! It's not. They'll tell you it's just a matter of keywords as well as buying content and putting it on multiple sites, including your own. The problem is, much of this content is almost always rehashed, rewritten or outright duplicated, and you'll get next to no credit with Google, at best. Actually, it cuts two ways: not only will you not *gain* any ground with Google, you'll *lose* ground because Google's algorithm will penalize you (dropping you down in its rankings) for sloppy content or content that is too keyword-laden. It's definitely not the way to go since you'll be falling behind your competitors if you try to take this easy way out.

Quality content has always been the centerpiece for being successful online, and that doesn't show any signs of changing. Creating quality content doesn't have to be hard, but it does take time, patience and discipline. There's a process to follow to ensure that you have the right kind of quality content that will get you ranked sky-high on Google. People have been trying to game the system with duplicate content and link farms for years, but Google has caught on to this sort of trickery. As a result, it's rapidly disappearing from the search engine landscape. Make sure not to get scammed by any of these offers – you know that if it seems too easy or cheap to be true, odds are that it probably is! Ask the company if their content is duplicated, rewritten or appears anywhere else; if they hem and haw before answering, run for the hills, and don't look back!

But you haven't gone to those other companies: you bought this book. With it, you've received the system and process you need that will, with some time, effort, patience and planning, get you to the top of the search results for your area.

⚠

Interviews From The Field:

Jonathan Fitzgarrald – JD
http://www.Greenbergglusker.com

What are the trends you see with Internet marketing and attorneys?

You have to understand that attorneys are risk adverse. They are not likely to be leading the market in social media or online efforts. The larger firms are able to take the lead, and in the past, smaller firms have taken direction from larger firms. That does seem to be changing. There has to be an incentive to spur change, and in the last several years, the legal industry has done really well. This means there has not been any outside pressure to do anything differently.

How important is it for firms to get on board with investing in their online presence?

With the Internet, new generations that have grown up on social media, the clients are forcing firms to change. If firms do not start communicating with clients on their level, there will be a dissonance between the firm and prospects. Getting online is something firms are going to have to embrace.

What are the barriers you see to getting into social media?

We have not seen too many barriers. For us, it starts with the leadership of the firms. There are states like Florida and Texas that have different standards regarding online marketing. Mostly, it depends on the law firm leadership and the marketing team at that firm. If you have someone like me that is pushing the firm to increase online presence, you will begin to see results.

Where have you seen the best returns of your time online?

We have seen our best results come from our blog. It is important to be present online in the area you practice. Instead of saying you are the smartest or best, showing that you have knowledge in an area helps demonstrate what you practice. Anyone can say they are great. Clients want to see some examples.

You should also have a well thought out profile on LinkedIn. For social media, LinkedIn is regarded as the professional space. We have gotten clients directly from LinkedIn that would have never found us otherwise.

Do you have a LinkedIn strategy?

Making sure that they have a good headshot, affiliations, resume and some strong recommendations on your profile. Potential clients search LinkedIn, and if you create a profile that clearly defines what you do, there is a good chance your name will come up when your prospect is searching for you. I also tell people to define their practice area in narrow terms as well as in broader terms. Making sure that you are specific to what you do as an attorney.

Back to blogging, what is your blogging strategy?

Ultimately, content is king! We make sure that we blog at least twice a month. If there are any current issues in our practice area people need to know, they can find that information on our blog. We suggest to our attorneys that they blog 2-3 times a week. These can be quick posts and should have some keywords, but we try to make sure that people avoid going too crazy with the keywords.

The point of the blog is for when people type in your keyword phrase, you come up on the first page in Google. You have to keep producing content to create those results.

Where do you see thing going in the future?

I see a huge trend towards firms interacting with their clients more often. This includes soliciting feedback, both positive and negative, to ensure that they are in touch with their clients' needs. Operating online is a great way for clients to connect with their firms.

What happens if people start saying bad things about you online?

It is possible that you will run into situations where people post negative comments about you online. Our strategy is to work on ensuring that we have positive feedback and information about us online. With our efforts, and since we provide a good service and build strong relationships, we are able to have more positive comments than negative. This is like a piggy bank...we put in a quarter every time a positive comment is made about us, either with a blog post, articles from our firm or comments online from a client. When a negative comment appears, it takes a quarter out. We are producing so much content, encouraging our clients to talk about us online and working to provide value, that we are adding dollars every week. If we have to take out a quarter every so often, we are still way ahead.

- While the Internet constantly changes, the stable principles outlined in this book won't steer you wrong.

- These online management principles will only work as well as they are implemented. Build (or find) a good team to help you implement strategies for online presence management.

- "Technology Alert" boxes will alert you to the upcoming changes we cover in the online section of the book—use them to keep your online presence updated!

- The yellow pages is breathing its last, and though you may think that the Internet isn't for you, the majority of your potential clients are looking for a local lawyer on the Internet—If you have no (or subpar) online presence, you'll be completely missed by potential clients searching online.

- Print, TV and radio advertising are seeing diminished returns on investment, making major investments in these mediums a waste. The Internet has a better return on investment than print, TV, and radio—*combined.*

- Google is the Internet's number one search engine, although many consumers also use social media and other search engines to find and information.

- All businesses—from small to enormous firms—can be found online through local search, which is what your firm should focus on—the first three local search returns (A, B, C) on Google garner more clicks than the rest of the entire page!

- With Google's local search and maps feature incorporated into their regular search page, businesses have a much greater chance of showing up high in search results—as long as they do a good job and follow the instructions in this book!

- This process is *not* easy, and beware of companies that tell you it is. Creating the kind of quality content and online strategy that gets you ranked takes time, patience and discipline, and if you try to game the system, Google will penalize you by lowering your website's ranking.

Notes

CHAPTER 2

Google:

Still King, Updates In 2012, and Other Search Engines

There is no question that Google continues to reign as king of the search world, with almost 70% of all search traffic. Bing, Yahoo! and other search engines all compete for the remaining 30% of search traffic. Though you've probably seen news coverage reporting that people spend more time every day, on average, viewing Facebook and other social media sites, it is essential to understand that Google's importance has not diminished: this is because, for now, Google search and Facebook serve very different functions. Even though people spend more time on average per day viewing Facebook, it is important to understand how and why people are spending time on social networking sites versus search engines.

Visiting a website like Facebook is typically done to review information that has been posted by your friends and family members. You may check Twitter for news or industry information and Google+ or Linkedin for work-related posts. When you visit Google, however, your only goal is to search for something and then immediately navigate to the webpage offering information on the subject for which you searched.

The average user searching for "Criminal Defense Attorney" or "Business Attorney" is going to get their search returns on Google within milliseconds, immediately move their eyes to the local returns (A, B, C, D and so on), then click the law firm that is ranked either A, B or C. This entire process might take 10 to 15 seconds at the maximum. If the user does not like the website they see on their first click, they will click the back button and most likely click the next search return. In total, every time a user searches for something, they are probably spending less than 25 seconds per search.

This is why being ranked high is so important and why having a site that keeps the person searching on the webpage is crucial (we will get to how you should design your page to keep people on your site later): the average user rarely clicks the search returns below A, B, C and D and clicks even less on the results on the next page.

The paragraphs below describe a few major changes that Google has made in the last year. Understanding these changes will help you make the appropriate strategy adjustments to maintain or gain a high ranking. Ignoring these changes will ensure your website falls further in the rankings over the next 12 months.

Major Recent Updates from Google:

The fact is, Google is constantly changing their algorithms to increase their effectiveness. This means that, several times every day, Google makes slight adjustments to how their search engine returns the best possible results when someone searches for something.

What generally happens much less often (but has dramatically increased in frequency this year) is that Google makes a major update. What constitutes a major update is both an announcement by Google of the update and, usually, a corresponding name to the update. Immediately after, you will see a shift in the search rankings of large amounts of websites. These changes are a positive thing for you, as an attorney. Why? Because each change makes it more difficult for people to cheat the system and get ranked without actually doing the work or being located in a specific geo-location.

Recently, we saw updates that included the Panda and, later, the Penguin Updates. Since you are mainly concerned with local search results, this information is geared towards getting ranked locally, as opposed to nationally—as mentioned In Chapter 1. Here is what you need to know as an attorney with regard to each update:

The Panda Update:

The Panda Update had a massive impact on overall search returns. The biggest change to local search in this update revolves around directory services and content farms that gain ranking by aggregating content from content originally written on other webpages and/or producing subpar content that is keyword-heavy. What this simply means is that certain websites were copying and pasting articles or writing content of no value to the reader—crammed with lots of keywords—and getting ranked because they had tons of content. Those websites no longer rank: only websites with unique and frequently updated, quality content are ranking highly.

With this update, Google was looking to prevent one company from receiving all the rewards from everyone else's hard work and to prevent companies from writing useless content just to get ranked. In a later update, the Penguin Update, Google really began to crack down on the practice of duplicate content.

What you need to know about the Panda update and your firm's web presence is simple: Google is requiring websites to produce useful, relevant and quality content.

The Venice Update:

This update flew under the radar last year, most likely due to the hysteria over Google's adjustments to the Panda update in versions 2.0 – 3.5. Interestingly, this impact was specific to local and should provide two major adjustments to your overall web strategy.

The first impact is that when you search terms like "Divorce Attorney" without a city location included in the search term, Google returns both the local returns A, B, C, D, etc. and local returns within the organic returns, both above and below the Google+ Local Listings. We've pointed out the changes, as also seen in chapter 1.)

(FIGURE 4 AND FIGURE 5)

The image above shows you the difference in local versus organic search returns. The organic search return (the one without the letter A, B or C next to it) is similar to a national search return. We will

FIGURE 4. GOOGLE VERSUS LOCAL RETURN

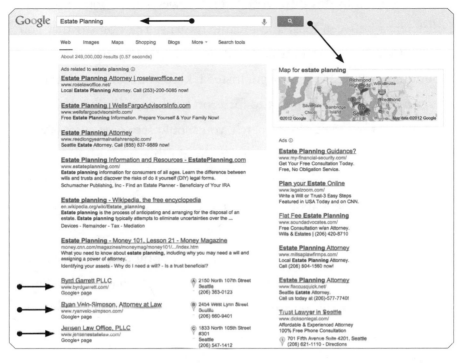

FIGURE 5. POINTING TO ORGANIC NATIONAL

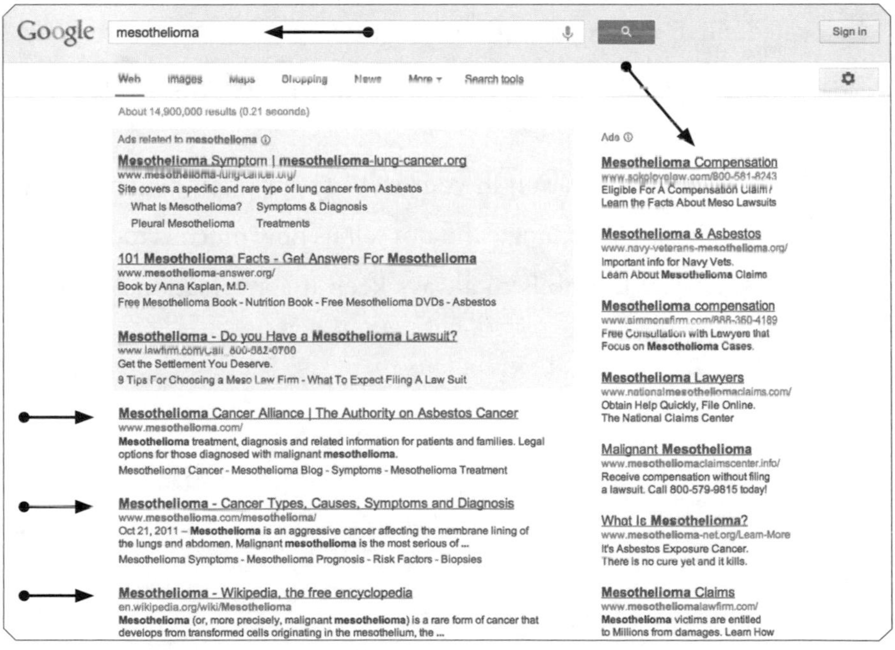

dive deeper into this difference later, but we wanted you to see the difference between local and organic returns. The point is that you do not want to start putting in all the time and money it takes to build a national SEO campaign. Instead, keep your focus on local listings (more to follow on how to focus on local, specifically). If you do things right with your local search, you should see some success with the natural organic results along with local returns.

There are a few great things this update made very clear to all website developers about how search engines want to see your address and location appear on the website:

You should include what is called a "Rich Snippet," similar to an h1 Card microformat on your website. This is a fancy term for adding your address in the hCard format of the coding of your website. (Something you should be asking your website developer to handle.)

Give written directions to your location on your contact page. This helps Google see a broader picture of where you are physically located. Give driving directions from two points of town to your office. If you have more than one office, give driving directions to each.

Overuse of your location in your website copy can be damaging to your overall ranking. Google did not tell us how much is too much, but a good rule of thumb is to always keep it conversational and as natural as possible.

The Penguin Update:

The most recent and most sweeping update since the Panda update, the Penguin Update has massive implications for local search returns… so pay attention because this is a big deal.

We mentioned that Google has changed its search algorithm, and one of those changes involves duplicate content. Because of the Penguin Update, it is now more dangerous than ever! The biggest reason duplicate content is so hazardous is that Google will give only one webpage "credit" for content that it finds across multiple pages. For example, let's say you have a Services Page on your website. On this page, you copy and paste the exact content from another firm's website. Google will only give one firm the credit for that content, and often, that credit goes to the person that posted first or the largest website. This means that you're not only getting zero credit towards your ranking but also wasting time on something that will not produce any results. That is time that you could have spent doing something that would add value to your web presence. There is a rumor that Google will be penalizing websites for duplicate content, but that has not proven to be the case—yet.

Another huge piece to the Penguin Update is the linking strategy on your website. This encompasses both inbound links and internal cross-linking (linking from one page on your website to another page on your website). This update provides a set of best practices regarding how, how often and when you should link within your own website as well as who you should be getting to link back to your website.

First, let's get the back-linking (aka inbound links) issue resolved. In short, a back link is anytime another website links back to your website. This can be a link to your website from the local chamber, a bar association, another blogger, etc. Back links are crucial to your SEO and one of the backbones of any good online strategy. At issue for Google and other search engines is the ease with which companies were able to game the system of back-linking through automated processes, building large networks where one company controls all the websites and through human capital.

To prevent companies from gaming the system, Google now grades the links that point back to your website and attributes that value toward your website's value. If all your back links are from websites that Google deems worthless, your website will drop in the rankings. How would this happen to a firm like yours? There are lots of questionable companies out there offering "cheap" SEO services. You have most likely gotten a call this week from one of them. The problem is, when a company offers great results for what seems like too good a deal, odds are they are cutting a few corners. One area they do this is by creating bad links back to your website.

Now more than ever, worthless back links are extremely damaging to your overall ability to get ranked: they will kill your web presence, so avoid them at all costs. We cover later in the book how to properly build back links to your website.

Internal linking is when you link from one part of your website to another. A common use of internal linking is your website navigation. You may have noticed that a lot of websites will also include the very same links used in the navigation in the footer of their website. The Penguin Update opens the door for the possibility of a penalty for adding these duplicate links to the bottom of your website.

Adding a link to most of your internal pages in the footer section of your website used to be a great way to boost your internal links.

You have likely seen this practice when scrolling to the bottom of a website and seeing a list of linked pages in columns. What Google has said is that your website navigation should be in one place, easy to use and preferably located at the top of the page. Now, why would Google care if your navigation links to the pages on your website are at the top of the page?

When you are ranked high on the first page of Google's search returns, Google is, in a sense, endorsing your website as the best option for that search term. If Google returns—and endorses—websites that are difficult to navigate, the user might start using a different search engine, like Bing, in hopes of getting a more useful and easily navigated result.

When someone searches for a keyword on Google and sees that you are the top return, Google wants your website to be easy to use and navigate for the person searching. This increases the amount of time the person searching spends on your website, which is something Google tracks. A person spending a lot of time on the website means that Google is doing their job: providing the best possible answer to that person's search query. It is well known in the website development community that navigation at or near the top of the website is the best place for optimal user experience.

The Penguin Update also began penalizing websites that have improper or poorly designed internal links from one page to the next. There are some web firms that cram as many links to another page as possible on one page. Google has said they would prefer, just as with links on the bottom of the page, that most of the internal linking be done within the navigation. Also included in this part of the update is Google's desire that there be unique names for each link. Instead of having 45 links on your website that all say "Adoption Attorney Sacramento, CA," Google would like to see both fewer links and something more relevant to the content surrounding the link.

A good example of this is the "About Me" or "Attorney Profile" pages. If you are speaking about an attorney at your firm and their specific practice area, it is okay to title your link "Adoption Attorney Sacramento, CA." However, if you are writing a blog post about adoption and you want to link to your adoption information page, make the link match the content:

> There is no fast track to adoption. Even though <u>adoption in the state of California</u> can take up to three years, it is possible to…

In the above example, the link would still be to the same adoption page as in the attorney profile page, but the name or text surrounding the link is more conversational in nature. It is not a requirement that the link title be conversational, but it is certainly an easy solution to this new best linking practice.

The same goes for images on your website. Too many websites were cramming their website with images that all contained the same keywords. If you are a divorce attorney in Denver, CO, then you need to make sure that the image titles read differently. It used to be common practice to title each image with basic keywords like "Divorce Attorney Denver, CO." Now, you want to include a description, such as "Family Going through Divorce in Denver, CO" or "Senior Divorce and Mediation Attorney in Denver, CO." Each image should have its own title that includes both your keywords and a longer description. This is more work but is worth the value added.

That sums up the most important changes and updates related specifically to attorneys. But that isn't everything you need to be thinking about.

Google has said many times, both verbally and in print, that it is striving to reward real local business that have quality and substance to offer to their community. As a result, they are cracking down very harshly on anyone who tries to game the system with shady methods, such as buying links or creating fake listings; both of these actions can get you delisted from Google's search index entirely and possibly for good. Have you ever tried to call Google's customer service line? If you have, you noticed there isn't a number to call. If your site is delisted, there is no easy way to get things back online.

Though this may seem harsh or unreasonable, remember that Google's effort to clean up its search engine only benefits you. You want them to go after the scammers and spammers so that you, a real attorney whose firm offers value and quality to consumers, can rise to the top—allowing people who are genuinely looking for your help and services to find you.

Other Search Engines:

We talk a lot about Google because they still get the lion's share of the traffic online. However, that doesn't mean you shouldn't also be thinking about the other search engines as well, including Bing, Yahoo! and even mobile search.

We will discuss Mobile Search in Chapter 12 because it is becoming a major source of website traffic and requires a very different set of rules than typical search. When it comes to every other search engine outside of Google, you need to know one thing only: do exactly what we are about to tell you to do in the rest of the book, and your website will begin to rise in the ranking of every other search engine as well.

That is great news for you. Other than Mobile, there is nothing more special than what we are about to tell you. There is no extra work, no tricks, no secrets: just one recipe for you to follow that will certainly lead to your online success.

- Google is king of all search engines, commanding nearly 70% of all search traffic, with Bing, Yahoo, and the rest competing for the other 30%.

- Although Facebook and other social media have become increasingly important, that doesn't mean that Google is any less important—more people search for businesses on Google than social media.

- Google constantly tweaks and sometimes makes major changes to their search algorithm to make search more effective for users and to thwart those trying to cheat the system.

- Recent major updates have cracked down on websites that have duplicate or subpar content, worthless back links, poorly designed internal navigation, and key-word-stuffed content.

- Engaging in spammy, shady practices (like buying links) to get your website ranked quick can put you at risk for Google lowering your ranking or delisting you from its search index *for good*.

- Don't just think about Google—optimize your website for other search engines, like Bing and Yahoo, as well as mobile.

Notes

Having a Pretty Website Does Not Equal Success!

So, now we know how important Google is; we've taken a look at how recent changes have impacted local search return and Google ranking, which are, in general, extremely important to your marketing efforts. We know that traditional media is fading fast and that if you want to stay on top of the game, you're going to have to get this search business straight right away!

The natural next step is to go and get ranked, and for that, you need a website. Your website is as much a part of this process as anything else. If you're going to get good conversions from your search rankings, you need a functional website that fully caters to both the needs of your firm and the needs of your clients.

> Traffic is important, but a website that has thousands of visitors and fails to convert them into real clients…is pointless.

The creation of a website can be a minefield, especially in today's whiz-bang, Flash-enabled, Web 2.0 world where everyone thinks that every website needs interactive menus, drop-down interfaces and all sorts of other bells and whistles. You see it all the time, in fact: people ask for "Web 2.0" or "interactive" websites, or developers try to push Flash this or Web 2.0 that on you, saying how important it is and how professional it makes your site look. And you may be tempted to believe them.

The truth, however, is this: for most small businesses and conversion rates, all of that fancy stuff does not matter. A solid, simple website will work far better at increasing your conversion and getting customers to contact you. This may seem counter-intuitive, especially in a world that seems to value style over substance, but it's true. Simpler websites have been far more effective at getting clients to call or email you than flashier, extravagant pages.

This does not mean you have to sacrifice design. You should still have a website that is professional and represents your firm well. The design should be professional, clean and functional. Mark Twain once said, "Sorry about the long letter, I didn't have time to make it shorter." And your website design is the same way. Creating a fancy website that has way too many functions is easy, but creating a simple website that maximizes your conversions takes time and energy.

This will seem a little daunting to add, in particular considering how much we've been talking about how important getting listed properly is, which still holds true: getting ranked high on Google still matters the most. In fact, the rest of this book following this chapter is devoted to that very concept. The website, however, is an integral part of the chain. It's by no means the most important link in the chain, not by far. Still, it needs to be done well, or it has the potential to ruin the entire concept of getting ranked on Google. The bottom line is this: if your prospect doesn't actually pick up the phone and call, all that effort you put into getting visitors to your site will have been wasted. No matter how flashy, how fancy, how up-to-date your website is, if there are no conversions, then that website is not working for you, plain and simple.

SO, WHAT DOES A GOOD WEBSITE LOOK LIKE?

OFTEN, ATTORNEYS ASK us, "What is the secret to getting visitors to pick up the phone and call?"

Before we jump into those details, there is a very important topic we must discuss: cheap-looking websites.

In today's market, there is no question that having a website is no longer an option: it is an expectation. If you have ever spoken with someone at a networking event or been told by a client that they would give your firm's name out as a referral, only to suddenly watch that prospect vanish, it is most likely due to a poorly designed website.

In your firm's office, you would not have a dead plant, broken chairs and a dirty waiting room. Your office should be professional, presentable and attractive. Well, guess what: your website needs to be a direct reflection of your office and your profession.

People searching for an attorney are holding you to a higher standard than the local dry cleaner. Having a website that looks like it was designed by your cousin's nephew in his parent's basement, circa 1998, is like wearing a suit with holes in the jacket to court. It is damaging to your professional image and flat out makes you look bad.

What makes for a well-designed site that actually converts traffic into prospects? There are a few things. Let's take a look at them and find out how to build the website that will get the most visitors to pick up that phone and call your office.

Site Construction:
What Should Your Overall Site Look Like?

In general, there is a rule that can be applied to websites looking to garner conversions from local search return: the less fancy the website is, the more conversions you'll get from it. Solid, functional sites will be far more effective for you. Keeping in mind that mentality, here is a general outline of what a sample website layout might look like:

- Home page
- About Us
- Practice Areas
- Special Report
- Blog
- Contact Us (with map and phone)

And that's it.

It might seem a bit *underwhelming* to you, as well as vastly smaller than the majority of the websites you've visited, and you're right. Those websites, however, are not ours. Your website should be lean and mean, built for one purpose and one purpose only: to get people who go to your website to call you or email you. Anything else is a waste; it's nice that people come to visit your site, but that doesn't mean anything for your business if no one calls or if you don't capture someone's phone or email for future follow-up.

Think of it this way: your website should not be cumbersome or difficult to navigate as this will cause people to get frustrated and leave your site.

We call it the 2-20-2-20 rule. You have less than 2 seconds to earn the prospect's next 20 seconds. In those 20 seconds, the visitors will determine if you earn their next 2 minutes. After that two minutes, the prospect will decide if they will call or email your firm and give you another 20 minutes to make them a client. What does the 2-20-2-20 rule mean for your website? You have to focus on the 2 seconds first to get to the 20 seconds. A simple, easy layout keeps a user's eyes on your website for more than 2 seconds. Cluttered, busy websites with way too many options or graphics decrease your chances of getting to the next 20 seconds.

Once you have those 20 seconds, every page should include a call to action. A call to action is something to get visitors to call you or email you right away. We'll talk more about the call to action later in the follow-up section, but just know that, at a minimum for local business websites, we recommend you include a banner or header that appears on every page; make sure your phone number appears in the top right-hand side or middle right-hand side. Studies show and our experience confirms that people's eyes gravitate toward the right side of a page—hint, look where Google puts their ads in their own search results.

Next, below your phone number and address, you need to add a form where visitors can sign up for your newsletter or special report by providing their name and email address. Other options that work very well in this spot include a form requesting an appointment or a place to ask a specific legal question. You can even put an image on the side that navigates to an online form. The reason this is so important is because some people may not be ready to call your firm, but you don't want to loose the opportunity to connect with them later. (FIGURE 6)

FIGURE 6. OPT-IN BOX

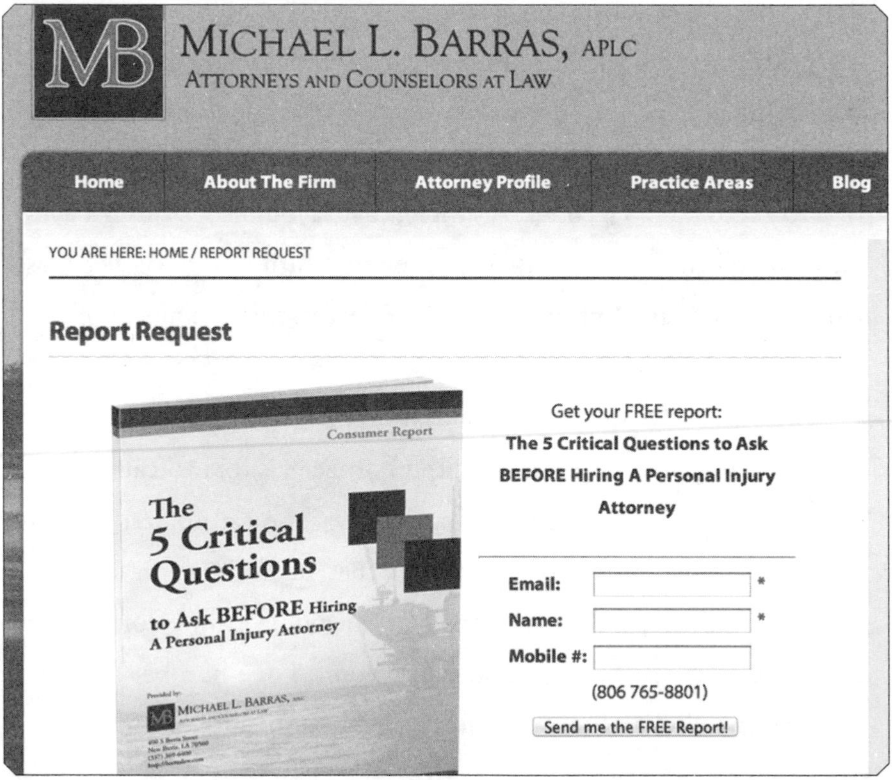

This is, of course, just an example: you are free to modify this layout however you wish. Depending on your firm, you may want to add a page about upcoming events you are hosting or recent news and press about your firm. Know, however, that this basic layout works extremely well, and always, always remember: the less fancy, the better the results.

Please do not confuse less fancy with bad design. You still want your firm and website to look professional, and we advocate a clean, simple design. In fact, we feel that having less 'flashiness' to a website often leads to better visual design because there is less clutter. A better visual design also helps with conversions. Your firm may have already invested in working with a branding firm to help create a logo and a set of colors that represent your "brand." If so, carry those onto your website. There are a number of color palette tools available online where you can enter your firm's core colors; they will provide you with suggested visually appealing, complementary colors. For example, there are: Colour Lovers (http://www.colourlovers.com) or Color Combos (http://www.colorcombos.com).

You are a valuable professional in your community, and your services are not (and should not be) cheap—don't let your website give potential clients the wrong impression. This means that you may not want to do it yourself and that you should be careful hiring the "webmaster" that operates out of his parents' basement.

NOW, LET'S BREAK DOWN EACH OF THESE PAGES MORE IN-DEPTH:

Home Page

There's not too much individuality going on here, but it's important for this page to connect your reader with the rest of the site. Make sure the page is easy on the eyes, has a blurb about you and invites the reader to explore more of the site. Above all, make absolutely sure that the home page features the blog prominently.

This is so important that I'm going to give it its own line: Make sure the home page features the blog prominently.

There are many ways to do this. Some firms have the actual blog on the homepage; if you don't want to do this, think very, very carefully about how to prominently integrate your blog with the home page.

Video is another important component for the homepage. Studies have shown a 60% or more increase in conversions when a visitor has the option to watch a video of someone from the firm on the homepage. Yes, that is 60%. Incorporate a small, short (30 seconds – 2 minutes) video somewhere on your home page.

THERE ARE SEVERAL ways you can create a video that won't cost you an arm and a leg. (Notice that the idea of setting up your own *camera is not an option.) Option number one is, of course, to hire a video production crew to film you. Create a simple ad in Craigslist that reads something like this:*

Request Title - Videographer Needed, ½ day, Plus Editing

Request Body – We are looking for a simple one-camera shoot to take place at our law firm. Please reply only via email with the following information:

- Do you have an HD camera and lapel microphone? (required)

- Do you have lighting? (required)

- Cost for shooting a 60 second video and some Q&A (approximately 2.5 hours of shooting)

- Cost for post production

=====End of request=====

Video continued:

From our experience, you should expect to pay somewhere around $500 for the whole project. The reason we add the Q&A portion to the video shoot is to give you content to use later. If you record a series of 10–20 questions and anrswers, you can chop the video up into sections and send them out to YouTube, post them on your blog or blast them out in press releases. If you have a video crew coming, you should take advantage of the opportunity as much as you can.

Of course, you will also need to have copy on your home page. For many attorneys, their home page reads like a biography of their best accomplishments. Does something like the following look familiar?

Smith, Smith & Smith Law Firm LLC was founded in 1987 here in any city, USA. Smith graduated from very-prominent-law-school in 1982, following three years of service in blank-organization. Smith number two graduated summa cum laude from another-very-prominent-law-school, and after spending two years as a clerk under very-impressive-judge Smith, won this-amazing-award.

You get the idea. While this is important information and includes accomplishments to be proud of, the home page is just the wrong place to put this information.

What you should be using instead is called Consumer Advocacy Copy. This is very important: when someone searches for the services that you provide, they are trying to solve a problem. This could be that they are getting divorced, maybe a loved one just passed away, or they might need help creating a contract for a great opportunity they discovered. The essential thing to remember is that they have a problem that needs to be solved, and your website should speak to the solutions they are after.

The copy on your home page should be about no more than 3 things:

1.   The benefits you provide someone (not your services or 'features' but the actual benefits clients receive as a result of working with you)

2.   Information about what is on your blog as well
      as links and enticements to good blog posts

3.   Call to action—what you can provide in ex-
      change for their call, email address or phone
      number: special offers, special reports, check-
      lists, etc.

These 3 items are so important to the success of a website that, for our private clients, we actually write these sections for them and place them word-for-word the home page.

Having a Law Firm Blog

Don't underestimate the blog: it's one of the most vital (if not *the* most vital) part of your website. It provides two things that are critical to your online success.

Your blog is the home to new and relevant content for your prospects to read; it is the place on your site where you should talk about all the things that are 'relevant' to your prospects and clients. You can discuss interesting things happening that affect your readers within your particular areas of law. If you focus on estate planning law, talk about trusts, powers of attorney, etc. You can also link out to a few recent news articles and provide some commentary about how they affect your readers. A hidden gem of relevant content that most firms overlook is local information. It doesn't have to pertain to law at all. If there is a big marathon, festival or parade coming up in your community, write a few paragraphs about the event with links to all the details in one place. If you know that parking is tough on Saturdays around the area, provide information about other parking; if there is a booth at the festival not to be missed, then tell your readers about that. You will be surprised that these will become your most popular blog posts: they build up your credibility as someone who lives, works and cares about your community.

Your blog is also a place for the search engines to crawl to find new and relevant content about what your firm does and where it provides those services. Everything we discussed above helps accomplish that; when talking about your area of law, you will naturally use the keywords that search engines will pick up. Furthermore, talking about things going on in the local community will help the search engines understand the community, town and cities that you should be associated with in the search results.

We hope that was simple to understand. Often, many marketing firms make this part too complicated. They talk about keywords, keyword density, latent search algorithms and more. It doesn't have to be that hard. Write about stuff that you know about and that provides value to your readers in a natural, conversational way. The two most obvious are your area of law and events going on in your community and nearby communities. If you hear someone talk extensively about keyword density and latent search algorithms, just run away: we think they are just trying to make it sound too complicated so that they can charge more.

This is so important that we hired writers to blog for our clients, which is something you could consider implementing at your firm. *That's* how important blogging is to us!

We will be discussing the specifics of blogs in a later chapter, from how many posts you should write to how you can find content from the web, fueling weeks' worth of writing.

(FIGURE 7)

FIGURE 7. BLOG

The About Us Page

The About Us page is, oddly enough, one that many firms get wrong. Often, attorneys are content to just throw in a short blurb about themselves or the partners and perhaps a map or two on how to get to the firm. This isn't enough information about you, nor is it helping you drive conversions. People care about your years of experience as a lawyer, yes, but that's not what's going to get them to call: it doesn't truly distinguish you from the other lawyers in the pack or give them a reason to give you their business. Instead, you have to think about something called a *"unique selling position"* or *USP:*

why do clients like to work with you and continue working with you? Information about you, your firm, why you're different, etc. and so forth just doesn't cut it. You have to show them why you're ahead of the pack and ultimately show them why they, as a consumer, want to work with you and not the other firm.

Think about it this way. Most people care about one thing and one thing only: WIIFM. That stands for "What's In It For Me." Your prospects could honestly care less about your degrees, titles or positions. Sorry. What they really want to know is if you can solve their problem… and solve it fast and professionally.

So, instead of talking about you, talk about them and why they will benefit from working with you.

That one tip alone, in fact, will set your website above and beyond most of the law firms we see: they simply don't set themselves apart sufficiently and, by doing so, you'll gain a very competitive edge in this field.

Contact Us

The Contact Us page should be very simple. You should have your email, your phone number, a map to your firm and written directions on how to navigate to your office from two places. That's it. You can perhaps put a slightly different or stronger call to action on this page, but for the most part, this page should be clean, simple and have nothing to distract the reader from picking up the phone or putting in their email. Some people add a contact form on this page. That is fine, but the most important thing is to provide a clear phone number or email that is directed and answered by an actual human. (FIGURE 8)

FIGURE 8. CONTACT US

CALL TO ACTION

SO, YOU'VE GOT the basic layout of your page all down. Just one thing left: your call to action.

What makes an effective call to action, and how can you put that to use on your site to generate those conversions?

An effective call to action is one that makes the customer pick up the phone and call right away or give you their email address. It is not one thing, one line or one strategy: it is a strategy that continues throughout your entire website. It's crucial that your call to action is very strong because you're asking for information that's become more and more private in modern times.

There are three ways to create a strong call to action that we recommend because we have tested them across hundreds of websites and know what works. And what works is asking prospects to take action: calling, requesting an appointment or providing an email address for future follow-up.

Getting People to Call Your Law Firm:

If you think that just because someone is looking for an attorney, they are going to dig around your website to find a phone number to call, you are sadly mistaken. People want easy access to the information they want, where they expect to find it.

What this means for you is that in order to get that phone to ring, you need to have a few elements in place. The phone number you use on your website needs to be the same number someone would get if they called 411 and asked for your firm's phone number. You should not use a 1-800 number on your website, unless it appears below your actual office number.

W A R N I N G

USING A TRACKING number on your website or anywhere online can have a dramatically negative effect on your rankings, leading to your website falling off the face of the earth. See the chapter about local directory listings for more information about your phone number and address. Never use a tracking number.

The first step is to put your phone number in the upper right-hand part of your website. This phone number needs to be text, not a jpeg image. Lots of web developers and companies will take the easy road and add an image of their phone number on the banner (or upper part) of their website. The problem is that a prospect cannot click on that image from a mobile device to call your firm. More importantly, search engines can't read images, so they'll completely miss your phone number. Make sure your number is easy to read on your website and on a mobile phone as well.

You should also put your phone number and address on the lower right-hand side of the website or at the bottom. This way, if someone is reading your website, scrolling down the page and ending up at the bottom with the inclination of calling you, your number is easy to find. At the point when someone wants to call you and give you their business (money), you should make this part of the process super easy.

The last place your phone number needs to be is on your Contact Us page. This is where you can add a fax number, extensions, your office number and any other numbers you think people may want to call.

Request an Appointment:

There is no question that this is the single best conversion technique on attorney websites right now. The best way to get a prospect to request an appointment is to put a box that is simple, clean and well-designed on your website. A nice bonus to the request an appointment box is that it can separate prospects into business you want for your firm and prospects you would prefer work with someone else.

Here is where your request an appointment box should appear: (FIGURE 9)

The box serves both as a filter and a great marketing tool. Ask the prospect to give you the following information:

- Name
- Email
- Phone
- Appointment Date Requested
- What is your case about?

The way this works is simple: a prospect fills out the form, selects a date and clicks schedule. Then, you or an administrator in your office receives an email with the person's contact information, date of requested appointment and details about his or her specific situation.

FIGURE 9. REQUEST BOX HIGHLIGHTED

This doesn't mean you have to meet with them at the time they requested. You can easily and professionally reply that you are not available at that time and give suggestions for another time. What is amazing about this tool is, since you ask for details, you get a chance to see if they are a good fit for your firm before you even talk with them on the phone. This will save you both time and money. If they are not the best fit, you can have your admin recommend them to someone else. If they are a perfect fit, you can set up an appointment right away. This really helps you prioritize these online leads.

After the prospect hits the schedule button, you should be re-directing (sending them) to a webpage that alerts them that their appointment request has been received and that you will contact them shortly.

Can I Please Have Your Email Address?

Sometimes people are not ready to contact you by phone, not in an appropriate place to make a phone call or not ready to schedule an appointment, but they may be interested in your firm. You don't want the prospect to close their browser and forget about you. This is an opportunity for you to capture their email address and reach out to them later, when they are more ready.

People know about spam, they know about scams, and they're hesitant to give out their email to just any site they find on the Internet. You have to overcome that initial hesitation and get them to give you their email. One way is to offer a special for providing information or calling now—like a big discount on a service. However, what we have that works the best is providing a special report about something that will be very helpful to the consumer who found you by searching for attorneys in your area.

Examples of this could be: "Special Report: 3 critical things you need to know before ever hiring or calling an attorney," "5 things you need to know before hiring a divorce attorney" or "3 myths you've been led to believe about Medicaid and Medicare." It's important that these examples be specific to your practice: the more targeted your examples, the more likely it is that you're going to get someone to sign up who wants to retain you as an attorney. You can make it even more targeted by making it local, for example: "5 things you need to know before hiring an attorney in Little Rock, Arkansas." These examples could be strong enough to get someone to put in their email. They might think to themselves, "What are those three things? I was ready to get moving and hire a lawyer tomorrow, but I better know this before I do anything" and pop in their email. Now, you can quickly follow up with them (and even automate some of the follow-up).

This content is so important, that, for our private clients, we write this report for them and place it on their website (after they review it, of course). The titles above take a "consumer advocacy" approach, which we found gets a lot more clients than more traditional lawyer advertising.

We also typically recommend that you ask not only for their email but for their cell phone number as well. People are giving out their cell phone numbers quite readily now, more so than a few years ago when it was very difficult to get someone's mobile number. Many people today use cell phones as their primary or even only phone number, and thus, they're more willing to give it out to people who ask if the reason is compelling enough.

If you follow all these steps, anyone who signs up with their email or phone number will be a "warm" lead: a "warm" lead is someone who's going to be very receptive to your business and much easier to convert into a client since they've showed a great deal of interest in your services; they've already done the hard part, which is getting in contact. You have to act on this, however: warm leads, like anything else warm, tend to cool over time, and if you don't act quickly, it'll be that much harder to seal the deal. This leads us to our next item of interest: follow-up systems!

It's vital that you have a stable, reliable follow-up system in place so that you can call a lead within five minutes of them submitting a form. If you can get to the prospect within 5 minutes, for example, you know they're an extremely warm lead, you know they were on the website, you know they were interested and you know they're looking for business. This is a much warmer lead than someone who just happened to see your name in a direct mail piece or in a local flyer.

There are some automated follow-up systems in place that are used by many firms: tools like Constant Contact, Infusionsoft and Instant Customer, among others. Depending on your area of law, there are some services that even provide dozens of pre-written email templates that have been proven to help convert email prospects into clients. One such company that provides this is NBK Marketing, LLC (http://nbkmarketing.com). If you want to use something like this, that's perfectly fine. But make sure to put the call to action form on that all-important right-hand side first. See the last image, and you will see exactly where this box should go on your website.

We'll talk more about follow-up later, in its own in-depth, complete section. First, however, let's get to the real deal, the heart and soul of this book—before you build that website, let's talk about getting your site noticed and getting it found so that search engines can send people to your site!

- To get found on Google by potential clients, you need a functional website.

- If your website doesn't convert visitors into actual clients, it's pointless!

- Simpler, more functional websites get more people to call or email than "flashy" websites. (Less fancy does not equal bad design.)

- Your website is your first impression online—a bad website is damaging to your firm's image and won't garner you any conversions. A good website is professional, functional, and attractive, not poorly designed, cluttered, or confusing to navigate.

- Your website layout should have a home page, about us page, practice areas page, special report, blog, and contact us page—and that's it.

- Each page of your website—and especially your home page—should use Consumer Advocacy Copy: copy that illustrates how you can solve a potential client's problem and how they can benefit from hiring you.

- Remember the 2-20-2 rule for earning your prospective client's time and attention on your website.

- Include strong calls to action on your website to get people to call or give you their information—your *real* phone number in the top right-hand corner as text, a request an appointment box, special offers, a special report, checklists, etc.

- Use follow-up systems to quickly get in touch with the prospective clients who've given you their information.

CHAPTER 4

Killing You Softly: Keywords.

Why You're Choosing The Wrong Words to Promote Your Firm Online and How You Can Find the Right Ones

Having a website is all well and good, but it doesn't do much for you if nobody visits it. You'll have to get Google to notice you and rank you highly, and you'll do this by using targeted keywords. We aren't going to make this a complicated discussion, but it is an important concept to understand.

What are keywords, you ask? Keywords are the words (either one word or multiple words) that users type into Google before they click search. A multiple-word keyword, like "Elder Law Attorney" or "Estate Planning Attorney," is called a "long-tail keyword phrase." When a user enters one of these keyword phrases into a search engine, such as Google, they will get back what Google thinks are the most relevant websites (or answers) to their search. Simply put, Google returns what it thinks are the best search results for the specific keyword phrase that the user entered in the search box.

That, in a nutshell, is the definition of a keyword. Within keywords, you will find two varieties: branded and non-branded.

Branded Keywords

Branded keywords are all the keywords that describe you, your brand and your proprietary products. These include your firm name, your personal name and the name of products you sell. For example, our firm may be called Homer & LeBret Law. "Homer & LeBret Law," "Mark Homer" and "Jabez LeBret" are keywords just like "estate planning" is because they describe something that may be searched online.

When people go to Google and type in your firm name (or personal name), they are obviously looking for you. They might be doing research about you or looking for your phone number, address or blog. The important thing to note is that they already know about you and are already looking for you. This means you do not need to, nor should you, spend much time or energy optimizing for branded keywords. When people search on Google for you by typing in your firm's name, Google will do a great job of ranking you on page one. Of course, this assumes your website is set up correctly—something we will walk you through in later chapters.

Non-Branded Keywords:

Non-branded keywords are all the keywords, both short- and long-tail, that prospects use to find answers online. This includes phrases like "criminal defense attorney" or "How long does alimony last?" These are the keyword phrases that you want to optimize for. We will discuss further on in this chapter how to find the best keywords and where to use those keywords. The key is to understand that these keywords drive your business. When you optimize for non-branded keywords, you are putting your website in front of people that do not know you yet and are searching for the services that you offer. If you are an adoption attorney, you want to rank on page one for the phrase "adoption attorney" in your local area. All your efforts should be focused on non-branded keywords.

WHEN YOU REVIEW your analytics or look at the report that your online marketing company sends you, take a look at the amount of traffic your website gets from branded versus non-branded keywords. You should see, over time, a steady amount of branded traffic and an increasing amount of non-branded traffic. This is what helps you determine if your web strategy is producing results. Are more people that are prospects finding your website versus the people that already know you? If the answer is yes, then your web strategy is working.

Your situation, however, is a tad more complicated than merely knowing what a keyword is: What keywords should you use? What keywords should you avoid? What keywords will get Google to notice that you are the best search result for a specific keyword phrase?

We have many firms who choose to have us do all of their Internet marketing for them. When we sit down at the table to discuss our plans for their Internet marketing strategies, there are two mistakes we see almost every time we start talking about keywords:

1) The first mistake we often see is that our new client will be very excited to show us that they rank #1 for their particular business name, like "Jones, Smith, & Partners LLC." So excited, in fact, that it's almost tough to tell them that it's nothing to be excited about: next to no one is searching for their exact firm name on the Internet. If they are searching for your firm name, it means they already know the firm and know what the firm does. They've probably been reached by one of your other marketing techniques, and you shouldn't be wasting any time positioning your firm so that the people who already know you can find you. In fact, these efforts are completely moot: Google and the other search engines already do a good job of making sure that your website ranks pretty high in searches of your firm name by people who search within 25 miles of your location.

Never forget: You're using the Internet to establish a professional reputation online and get *new* customers who are looking to solve a problem that you and your firm can solve; in short, you need to present an attractive solution to people with problems. People need help with things like "veteran's benefits," "long-term health care," "divorce advice" or "real estate issues." These are the keywords people put into the search box! New prospects are not looking for "Jones,

Smith, and Johnson LLC"—they're looking for "estate planning" or "long-term health care," things for which an attorney can provide a solution. You want to rank for these types of keywords. Understand that when you do everything else right, you will automatically rank for your business name.

2) The other big mistake we see made all the time is ranking for terms that only make sense to someone who works in that particular industry. One instance of this that we've seen lately is the keyword phrase "Elder Care Law." Not many people know that elder law is an entire area of the law industry; though they might learn about this term and start searching for it in the future, they're not doing so in great numbers right now. (Google provides data about what people are searching for, and, while sometimes confusing to interpret, the data is free). What the ideal Elder Care Law prospect is typing in is "How can I afford long-term care," "How can I afford the nursing home," "How can I get veteran's benefits" or even "estate planning." People may not understand the terminology "Elder Care," but they do have a general idea that estate planning might be what they're trying to look for. What they're really looking for is someone to help with their own or their parents' VA benefits or Medicaid.

It is crucial to remember in keyword selection that you must look at keywords from the user's perspective. You can't expect users to search for the terms you don't believe they're going to be able to define. For example, don't go to your industry association definitions for keywords, unless it's to see which keywords not to use. It's a trap that many people fall into all the time, and you've got to watch out for it. Even we're not immune to it; we deal heavily in search and social media Internet marketing, and when we're not careful, we find ourselves using terms people wouldn't use and don't care about: "Website Optimization" or "Social Media Measurement." These are things our clients would never type into a search box online. Instead, they would type in something like "Law Firm Marketing," and so those are the keywords we really care about.

These are the two big pitfalls in keyword selection that we see happen to most firms that we work with, and they both stem from one thing: a lack of knowledge—specifically, a lack of awareness of what people search for. There are a number of tools available online to find out what people search for, in addition to the free Google tools.

For a complete list of online research tools, go to the link below. Since these tools often change, it is important that you have the most up-to-date information. Once there, you will find our most current listing of tools you can use to research your market and keywords.

Go to...

www.GetNoticedGetFound.com/keywordresources

These various online tools are helpful, and clients who know how to use them will really benefit from the services they provide. However, the best and possibly quickest way to think about finding the right keywords is to just ask your family and friends. Think back to the first chapter, when we said that ordinary people use Google—that's as true for keyword usage as it is for research methods. Ask your friends, colleagues outside of the law industry and neighbors for help; ask people you know to explain what your firm does as if they were telling a friend. They will use terms in plain English to describe your business, and those are the terms that ordinary people are going to type into the search box.

The reason this works is because it gets into the mind of a client. If you gave a 60-second description of what you do to a client, and they turn around and tell that to a friend, it's not going to sound the same; in fact, it'll likely be very different! What you're looking for in keyword selection is not how you describe your own business; it's how clients and prospects describe it. If you're not ranking on the keywords that people are searching for, nobody's going to find you.

This might be a little overwhelming, but don't worry. We're not saying that you have to nail this on the first try or that you can't ever change keywords over time. It's not the end of the world if you choose the wrong keyword on Day 1: keywords can be modified, refined or even completely switched out altogether. Don't overthink your keyword selection to the point that you freeze. Start off by asking your neighbors and friends, as we described above. This is a very good method to find initial keywords, and as you get more advanced, you can start using some of the tools we talked about above to refine your keyword selection. (Those tools will definitely benefit you, but they're not crucial right out of the gate.) Start simply and slowly grow in complexity as you master each step of the process.

Interviews From The Field:

Edmund Scanlan, CEO of Total Attorneys, http://www.TotalAttorneys.com

How did you get into marketing for attorneys?

I built my first website for my father, who is an attorney, in 1997 for his practice. From there, I went and worked for the non-profit United Away, writing a comprehensive plan for what their website should be. From there, I worked for several firms until 2000, when I launched my own firm where I found myself working more and more with attorneys. Now, I am CEO of Total Attorneys.

What does your firm do?

We are a full web-based solution for attorney's offices. We also offer a 24/7 answering service for attorneys that may not have the resources to hire a full time person to sit at a front desk. Our systems work with the attorney on tracking time, managing documents and handling clients. It also has portals for clients to obtain information and interact with the attorney.

What trends have you seen over the last 5 years?

Years ago, they wouldn't believe people were looking for attorneys online. There has been a big shift with regard to getting on the web. There is still some confusion about how to enter the online space, and with so many companies out there selling products, there is a lot of white noise. A few years ago, I was going to meeting after meeting talking to attorneys about why they needed a web presence. Now, there is at least a shift to understanding that you need to be online. There is just confusion about how to be online.

How does a firm apply branding to their online presence?

Back in the day, it was customary for firms to brand themselves with their last names. You are starting to see more law firms talking about what their clients' issues are and less about what makes them feel warm and fuzzy. Most consumers don't really care what year you graduated from law school. Clients are usually looking first to find a solution to their problem. Then, they are going to dig in with the details of the firm.

Are you seeing push back from attorneys on using social media, blogging and other marketing mediums?

The biggest issue is attorneys don't have time to manage a multi-channel marketing effort. Which is really what is happening. Things are getting more fragmented, not less fragmented. You used to be able to work with a company that handled one thing; now, you need to find a marketing firm that understands how to manage social media, reviews, etc. It is not that it is overly complicated; it just takes too much time.

How is this different for attorneys?

Since an attorney needs to be doing the attorney work, drafting legal documents etc., they can't be managing marketing campaigns that take up 1/3 of their day. Other markets can hire people to handle the tasks, like a coffee shop owner can hire another barista easily. An attorney does not have that option. So, they need a simple solution that takes care of the multi-channel marketing campaigns that you need to have in today's market.

ANOTHER IMPORTANT TOOL in your keyword research arsenal is the Google Keyword Tool (GKT for short). The GKT is important because, although the Related Searches tool gives you suggestions, the GKT gives you returns for how many people per month are actually searching for a certain keyword. This data is given across the entire

U.S., so you'll have to make the educated (and usually valid) assumption that the keywords will work in your locality very similarly to the way they work nationally. To stick to our earlier example, let's type in two terms: "estate planning attorney" and "elder care law."

(FIGURE 10)

We are going to compare two keyword phrases, even though you can target between three to five. You'll notice in the screenshot above that "estate planning attorney" gets almost three times as many searches as "elder law attorney." In fact, "elder law attorney" receives such a small number of searches, comparatively, that you may not even want to initially target it. (You would want to check "Veterans Benefits" or "Medicaid Assistance.")

You can assume that, in your locality, these numbers will probably translate fairly well. It's not a given, but since there isn't a great tool currently available to pinpoint exact numbers of local searches, you need to assume that the national numbers will more or less apply reasonably well to your local searches.

If you really want a good idea of how many local searches those national numbers signify, you can do a rough calculation: take the last census date for the total U.S. population, and take the census of your location (within approximately 25 miles). Divide your local population by the total population, and you'll get a rough estimate of your area's percentage of the total population. Then, multiply that number by the number of national searches of a keyword to get the number of local searches (in your area) of that keyword.

$$\frac{(local\ population)}{(total\ population)} = \begin{array}{c} \% \ of\ your\ local\ population\ to \\ total\ population \end{array}$$

Figure 10. Google Keyword Tool

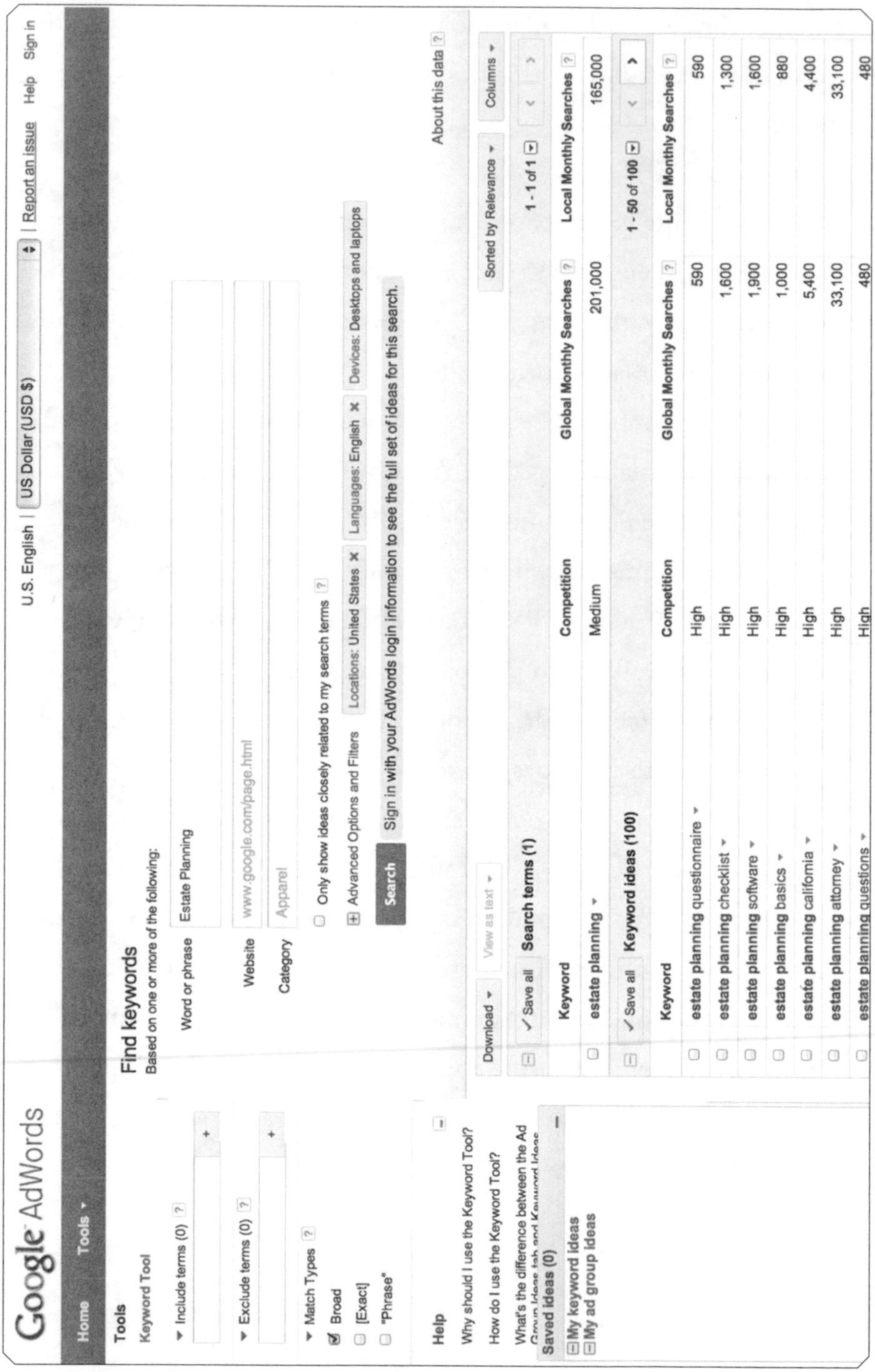

% of total population

X = *# of local searches*

# of national searches

For example: Let's say you live in a city/area with one million people. The U.S. has 300 million people, by last count, which means your city has 1/300th the amount of searches. "Estate planning attorney" returns 300k hits per month, so we can assume that your locale receives about 1,000 searches per month on that keyword. It's not exact, but it's a very good estimate—often more spot-on than you'd expect!

City: 800,000

US: 300,000,000

Monthly Traffic: 201,000

800,000 / 300,000,000 = .0026667

201,000 x .0026667 = 536 **searches in your city**

every month!

Now, think about your conversions. Let's say that you only convert ½ of 1 percent of those people searching online into clients. That would equal 2 new clients every month from your website. For most firms, adding 2 new clients that did not come from referral, networking or word of mouth but came because they found you online is a great bump in business.

That's just the result of one keyword phrase. A well-planned campaign should get your business ranked for at least 3 phrases, each with their own traffic numbers. With the strategies we lay out in the following chapters to help you convert this traffic into new clients, you are going to see results that may lead to you hiring more people.

These kinds of results do not happen overnight or in one month, and, in fact, you don't even want them to happen that fast. You want the kind of online web presence that produces great results over an extended period of time, not just one month and done. In order to produce these long-term results, you need to build a very large, sturdy and well-rooted online foundation—and that is what this entire book is about.

Do not think that bigger is always better! This means that you should not think that the more competitive keywords are always better. Sometimes, it's better to go after an easily dominated keyword. Think long-term instead of flashy.

Another pitfall that companies succumb to is that they typically want a neat, catchy name or their firm name in the URL. If you want to rank really well, you're going to have to make your URL keyword-rich. Not too long ago, we would have recommended this strategy; in fact, here is an exact excerpt from our previous edition of this book outlining what is no longer a proper strategy.

~~Here's an example: Let's say you're an attorney in Dallas, Texas, and you've decided on the keyword phrase "estate planning attorney Dallas TX". A great URL for your website, then, would be "http://www.EstatePlanningAttorneyDallasTX.com". That's going to help~~

~~tremendously in your efforts to rank high on Google. We realize that~~ ~~that's not a pretty name, and if you want to have your firm name~~ ~~website URL for business cards and marketing materials you still can.~~ ~~It's both cheap and trivial to have multiple domain names, and you~~ ~~can easily have your webmaster redirect "http://www.johnsonand-~~ ~~smithllc.com" to "http://www.estateplanningattorneydallastx.com"~~ ~~and still reap the benefits of the keyword-rich URL while having a~~ ~~professional URL on your business cards.~~

A keyword-rich URL is no longer a strategy that works. It may be easier to remember for prospects, but it *can* have a negative effect on your rankings. The text above is the actual text from our previous version of this book. We left it in and crossed it out to demonstrate the importance of keeping up on the changes that are constantly occurring in the online world. We have included in this book several places that offer more resources on our blog. Because technology changes so rapidly, we want you to be as informed as possible.

Do not panic if you already have a keyword-rich URL. Google just recently began a campaign to clean up their search results, specifically targeting keyword-rich URLs. Since this recent change has not been in effect long enough to provide actionable advice, we recommend you turn to Google to find out how you can avoid any punishment. Just Google the phrase "Keyword Rich URL Positive or Negative," and do some research. You may also want to head to YouTube and watch some videos by Google's Matt Cutts.

NICHING

WITH THIS KNOWLEDGE comes another facet of Internet marketing you need to be familiar with: niching. As you may have already guessed, you can't be highly ranked in everything. Unless you're a general practice attorney in a small town, there will be a crowd of other attorneys vying for the same top spot for many different keywords. To stand out, you're going to want to select some specialty or niche to focus on.

This isn't to say that you can't do other things or cross-sell once you get your client, but you definitely have to step back and strategize when it comes to niching. Where is most of your revenue coming from? Where do you want it to come from? What's your most profitable set of clients?

Some areas require a significant amount of senior attorneys' time, while there are other things that senior attorneys can review and have paralegals do most of the actual work: the second is often more profitable.

What it comes down to is this: To dominate online, you have to know where you want to go and focus on one thing. Choose something that you'd be happy with if 95% of your business came from that one thing. What is it? This is where you're going to want to start in regard to your keywords. Dominating the search rankings under elder care, personal injury, estate planning, divorce, DUI and so forth, all at once, is going to be really difficult, if not outright impossible. Start with the most important one, the one where you most want to go (even if it's not where you started): the niche that you want to dominate in the future. Dominating that one keyword phrase means owning that particular source of business in your area.

Another extremely important aspect of this strategy is determined by whether or not you're in an area where someone else is already dominating a larger keyword phrase. If another firm or attorney is dominating the keyword phrase you want, you can always focus on smaller subsets of that keyword phrase: if you can dominate 2 or 3 smaller keyword phrases, you may end up actually getting more business than the company that just went after the larger, broader term.

In keeping with our earlier elder care example, let's say you want to dominate the keyword "veteran's benefits."

Once you've narrowed down between 3-5 keyword phrases, you'll want to make sure those keyword phrases are in the part of your website called the "title tag." This is something you will want to ask your webmaster for help with. The order is very important: you want the title tag to start with the keywords, move into the location, and end with the business name. Don't lead with your business name; the business name will come along for the ride. It's all over your website, and people (and Google) aren't going to miss it. Instead, start with the important keywords, and make sure those are peppered all throughout your site. For example, you may put "Trusted Veteran's Benefit and Estate Planning Attorney in Portland, OR | Smith and Smith PLLC."

W A R N I N G

DON'T OVERDO IT! Google is looking for real people with real content, not automatons who simply spew out keywords nonstop. There's a joke in the Search Engine Optimization world about this:

Q: How many Search Engine experts does it take to change a light bulb?

A: Light. Bulb. Light bulb. Lamp. Fluorescent. Incandescent. LED. Flashlight...

The joke is light-hearted, but the message is clear: don't over-saturate your website with keywords! Make sure your keyword density (the number of keywords per 100 words) hovers around 4% in the page text, which is the optimal percentage for keywords to words. (Okay, we said we wouldn't try to confuse you with terms like keyword density, and we just brought it up—but you know the specific data now, if you choose to use it. However, you can also simply stick with talking about your subject in a natural way, and this will just work itself out.)

Another extremely important aspect to think about in this strategy is whether or not you're in an area where someone else is already dominating that larger keyword phrase. If another firm or attorney is dominating the keyword phrase you want, you can always focus on smaller subsets of that keyword phrase: if you can dominate 2 or 3 smaller keyword phrases, you may end up actually getting more business than the company that just went after that larger, broader term.

All the knowledge in this book is important to understand for an attorney because it enables you to create your own online strategy—for keywords and beyond—or be savvy when you hire a firm to do it for you. If you hire an outside firm, you'll be able to make sure it's not just a webmaster who puts up a quick website but somebody who will ask the tough questions and really help you to think through the right online strategy for you. Just like the duplicate content we mentioned in Chapter 1, there are lots of people just trying to sell something quick and dirty, instead of doing things the right way. So, don't get fooled or go into any negotiations without knowing what an online marketing firm should provide you.

Once you've got your keywords, your domain name and your website ready, it's time to step up your game: we're going to get into blogging to get ranked and more advanced local search techniques!

- A website won't do anything for your business if no one finds it!

- To get Google to rank your website highly—where you will be most visible to potential clients—you need to use the right keywords.

- Keywords are one word or multiple word phrases that users type into Google's search box. (e.g. "criminal law attorney"). Google returns the search results that it thinks best matches those keywords.

- If you rank for the keywords that nobody searches for, no one will find you.

- When choosing keywords that you want to rank for, remember that it's not really important to focus on ranking for your firm name and that you don't want to rank for keywords using legal jargon (which the average person doesn't use).

- Choose your keywords from a user's perspective (ask your friends and family how they would describe what you do). What are people searching for online, and how can your firm provide a solution to their questions and problem?

- Remember that the keywords you try to rank for can always be tweaked or swapped out altogether—they're not set in stone.

- You can't dominate every keyword: sometimes, it's better to rank for a less competitive keyword (or a subset of the competitive one) or rank for a keyword in an area where you'd like to get more business.

- Use your keywords in your website copy and in your website title tags, but DON'T stuff your keywords into every nook and cranny of your website! Your use of keywords should be natural and readable—remember that an actual human being is going to read your content, not just Google!

Notes

CHAPTER 5

Let's Get Local:
Advanced Local Search Techniques

I f you've been following this guide thus far, you've got a pretty reasonable setup started. In fact, you're probably better off than anyone who has simply thrown together a website to create an Internet presence, and you're definitely better off than anyone who has refused the transition to web-based marketing. You may have even pulled a lead or two just from having the website, and you're now considering putting your Google Plus Local (Google+ Local or g+Local) page up right away to watch your site skyrocket to the top of those local search returns for even more potential business!

We like your initiative, but hold your horses: your site's still small fry. In this chapter, we're going to help you figure out how to make your firm a big-time local business on the web by using several more advanced local search techniques. For those firms that have multiple locations, read this section first, and we will cover multiple locations following this chapter.

When you search for your firm on your own computer, you will get skewed results because you visit your website more often than your prospects. Google pays attention to where you search and, if you search your own firm often, will return your website higher in search returns than it actually appears to someone else in your own city. Also, searching from outside your city location will skew your results. If you want to know where you rank locally, you should have someone you know from your city who has never visited your website search for your keywords. From this, you will see where you truly rank.

First, let's define the difference between local and national search. There are actually tons of places you can get ranked on Google and other search engines. There are paid advertisements or PPC, national rankings, local rankings, social search ranking and local organic. We are going to focus on local rankings.

(FIGURE 11)

In the image above, you see exactly what we are talking about. The local search rankings are the lettered rankings that correspond with the map on the upper right. It may be difficult to remember, but

FIGURE 11.
GOOGLE SEARCH WITH LOCAL A,B,C SLOT HIGHLIGHTED

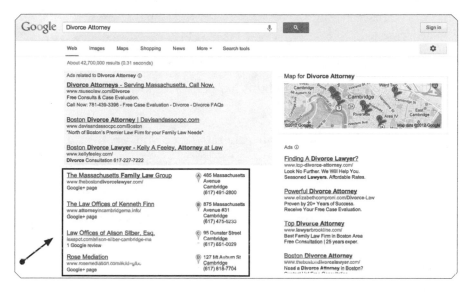

not too long ago, this map did not appear on the first page of Google. In fact, you had to navigate to the Maps page to even see the local results. It is estimated that Google lost over $3 billion when it put that map on their main search page. Why? Because that map covers up their top three ads, their most valuable real estate on their website: the upper right-hand corner. (You will recall in the conversion section that we discussed putting your request an appointment box in the upper right-hand corner of your website for this very reason: it is where people look first.)

It was in October of 2010 that we began to see this map appear on the main search page. This major change in focus is what has opened a huge door of opportunity for your firm because getting ranked locally on that map and within the A, B, C ranking on the main page of Google is drastically different than ranking on a national scale.

The reason ranking local is so important is because, when people look for an attorney, they look for one in their home town, near where they live or work, so they can meet in person and shake their hand. This is you: you are a real human being in a real city, as opposed to some directory service. You should be in front of people looking for your services, and this happens with local, in comparison with national, search.

At this point, Google will generally give you up to a 25-mile radius from your office location. This means that you can appear in search results on prospects' computers up to 25 miles away from your office. This is not always the case: In more densely populated cities, that radius shrinks significantly. Take Seattle, for example. We have a client located in the Ballard area of Seattle. Their address to the office is Seattle, if you asked them, they would tell you they work in Seattle, but if you are from Seattle, you know that Ballard is its own place.

Google also considers Ballard to be a unique geo-location. You can actually set your city location on your search to be "Ballard Seattle, WA" and get returns for that exact area.

This is important for anyone in a larger city, like Chicago, San Francisco, Denver, Boston, New York, Miami, etc. Your first goal is to get your firm ranked in your exact location. Try searching Google with your actual location, like "Business Law Attorney Lincoln Park Chicago IL" and see if the results vary compared to "Business Law Attorney Chicago IL." If they do, and I suspect they will, you know there is a micro-location to the larger city.

When you have established that there is a smaller location to the larger area, begin adding your neighborhood name in your keywords.

This will help you further narrow down, to Google, exactly where you are.

Getting Ranked In Your Local City or Another City:

A statement we get all the time from firms that are looking to have us get them ranked locally is "I want to rank in my city and the city next door." Here is what Google and all the other search engines have said about your location and getting ranked:

You are supposed to pursue and establish the location that is your actual physical location. Imagine if I were to call 411 directory information and ask for your address. What address would they give me? That is the address that Google wants you to use and is the address they will rank you by.

For some firms, it is important to rank in cities other than their physical location, and here is a simple (and pretty much the only) work-around to this location conundrum: rent a temporary office space in another city. You cannot rent a P.O. Box or use a shared mailbox drop, even if that drop box gives you a suite number. Google knows that the Mailbox, Etc. is not a real office, so do not try to fool them.

What Google is trying to accomplish here is to have real businesses be able to get ranked in their local city. This is a great thing for your firm. If anyone could get ranked locally without having a real office space, then companies would game the system, dominate the rankings, collect all the leads online and then sell those leads. This type of behavior used to happen; in fact, it even happened in the legal industry. Companies would rank high on search terms, make prospects fill out online forms and sell those leads to attorneys. Google decided to cut out the middle person and let the prospect go directly to you.

Core Components to Getting Ranked Locally:

Here is a list of where you need to focus to get ranked locally: website optimization, directory services, links and your blog.

Your blog and directory services are so important that we dedicated entire chapters to those. How often to blog, what to blog about, how to fill out directories online – we answer all that in future chapters. For now, let's focus on website optimization and links.

Website Optimization:

Establishing the right keywords and knowing what terms rank for local search is key. Remember that your keyword phrase should include your location when you type it onto your website (for example, "Adoption Attorney Charlotte, NC"). Once you have the right keywords, you need to start using them on your website. Your website optimization occurs in several places, both visible and invisible to the user; certain things you will do to help Google "see" where you are located.

The first place you need to optimize is your title tag. We discussed this earlier, but it is worth mentioning again because it is the first thing Google sees.

The copy on your home page should include your location and keywords. If you are writing good consumer advocacy copy, you will want to casually drop (once is enough) on your home page your keyword plus your location(s).

Your address should appear in text in the upper right-hand part of your website along with your phone number. **An image will not be acceptable here:** it must be text in your banner in order for the search engines to be able to see it. Sometimes you have multiple offices and may want to list your phone numbers in the upper right corner and put your address on the bottom of the home page.

(FIGURE 12)

Your address should appear on the bottom of the page, as mentioned in a previous chapter, and also on your contact page.

In addition, embed a Google Map with your specific location onto your contact page. This is a great way to signal to Google that your website is connected with that specific address.

In order to make sure that Google and other search engines are able to connect your address with your website as quickly as possible, you will want to add what is called Rich Snippets to the code of your website. Do NOT attempt to add this yourself unless you know how to program websites. Ask your webmaster to add an Rich Snippets for your address and phone number. If they do not know what that is, you are working with the wrong firm. This is not something that people can see when they are looking at your website; it is something just for the search engines.

Another element just for search engines, something less important compared to what's above, is adding your geo-location to your meta tags and website description. This is also something people

FIGURE 12.
WEBSITE WITH PHONE NUMBER AND ADDRESS HIGHLIGHTED

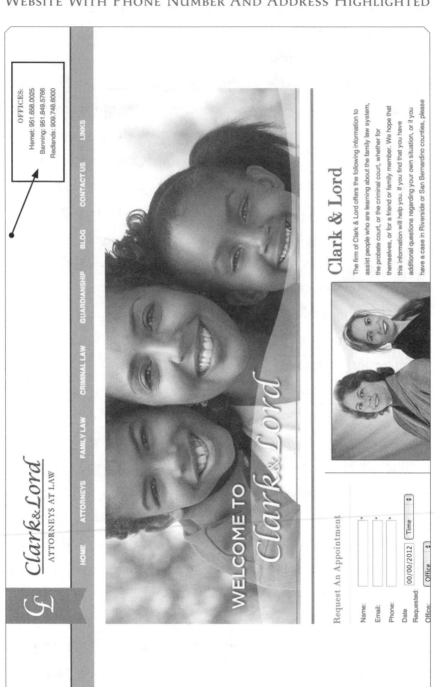

cannot see and is something you should have your webmaster take care of for you.

ADVANCED TIP: If you are ready to get really advanced on your website optimization, here is a technique that our friend Michael Dorausch @chiropractic (http://Twitter.com/chiropractic) shared with us at a recent tech conference where we were both speaking: add images to your website that are geo-tagged. How this works is not simple, but it is something that can be done and is something we guarantee your competition is not doing. To do this, find a camera that automatically tags images with your exact geo-location via GPS. Take photos of your firm, your neighborhood or city and events that happen near your office.

Now, set up an account with Panoramio (http://Panoramio. com,), a photo sharing application Then, gather those images that are going to appear on your blog or your website and upload them to Panoramio. Now, take the images that you uploaded to Panoramio and embed them onto your website.

What is happening here is your image is going to send a concrete signal to Google (Google owns Panoramio, by the way) that you are located in this specific geo-location. It is not that Google doesn't know where you are located; instead, what you are trying to accomplish is sending stronger signals than your competitors.

- Local search is *much more important* that national search for law firms, because people look for an attorney in or near the town where they live or work! This is why you want to rank in the top three spots (which people click the most) of Google's local map search results.

- You can get ranked on Google in your firm's location and up to a 25-mile radius around it—depending on the size of your city. You CANNOT get ranked in a city where you don't have a physical office, unless you rent a temporary office space.

- To get ranked locally, focus on website optimization, directory services, links and your blog.

- To optimize your website, use your location and keywords (in a natural way!) in your website copy, title tags and meta description.

- Your address and phone number should be placed in the top right-hand corner of your website, at the bottom of your page and on your Contact page—along with an embedded Google map.

- Ask your Webmaster to add h1 microformatting to the code of your website for your address and phone number to make them stand out to Google.

- Advanced tip: Add your geo-location to images to strengthen your website's location signal to Google.

Notes

CHAPTER 6

Content Is King:

Blogging, Press Releases, and Videos

G oogle has made one thing clear: you must have quality content if you want to get ranked. Content comes in many forms, from articles to videos. Some old techniques in internet marketing no longer work, like articles, while other types of content, including press releases, videos and blogs are working great for improving your ranking. This chapter is going to dive into one of the most important and time-consuming pieces of building a successful web presence.

Often, we are asked how an attorney is supposed to know what content to create. As Google makes algorithm changes, those changes create a road map for how search engines are deciding what websites to rank and why. The recent changes made over the last year, plus several industry updates by Matt Cutts from Google, have clearly shown that what search engines are looking for is quality content created on a regular basis.

Back in the day, 15 years ago, you could just cram a ton of your keywords on your website and get ranked. Then, search engines started looking for other indicators, including links to your website from other websites (back links). When Google first launched, they relied heavily on back links to determine a website's worthiness. The more links you had, the better chance you had of getting ranked.

Things have since completely shifted in how you get ranked. This is not to say that back links are not important, but having great content is more important than ever. There are certain key types of content that Google and other search engines are looking to in order to determine your website's worthiness to be ranked high.

Those types of content include press releases, videos, social media content and blogs.

For different types of businesses, we recommend different content strategies. For attorneys and law firms, the most important content you can create is in the form of a blog.

Your Blog:

You have to have a blog on your website. There is no option. Google has emphatically stated that they're going to give stronger ranking credit to resources that are both relevant to the website and most current. This makes sense, given the overall makeup of the

Internet: new content is replaced often, and newer information is frequently far more useful than old information to a person searching.

There are several ways a law firm can use a blog. It is possible to create a blog, attract readers and establish yourself as someone that is very knowledgeable about your practice area. Realistically, to dominate a market with a blog and establish yourself as the go-to person in your attorney niche, you will need to invest about 20 hours a week into this blog. Let's get real; you should not have an extra 20 hours a week.

As an attorney, you should be focusing on two purposes for your blog: increasing your ranking and providing depth to your website.

Your blog needs to be on your website. It should not be a separate URL or a completely different website. We have seen several law firms that have a main firm website, and clicking on their blog, takes you to a separate website. Since blogging sends signals to Google and other search engines that your website is both current and relevant, you want all the credit from your hard work to promote your main website. Having a website and a separate blog is like having a car without an engine. It may look like a car that could drive you places, but ultimately, it is not going to get you anywhere.

It is true that blogging has become the online activity-du-jour on the Internet, and it seems that everyone and their cat has a blog. (In fact, some people have several.) However, that doesn't detract from the fact that blogging has become a powerful force on the Internet. It also has a distinct advantage for your law firm in that it's by far the easiest, most convenient and most effective way to add new, updated content to your website. You don't have to change your website copy all the time, you don't have to deal with static pages, HTML and minor edits; you just have to update your blog consistently.

Also, blogs are especially helpful when you consider Google's other preference in high-ranking search results: steady, relevant content. There's no "magic bullet" or fast-track way to get to the top of the Google's search rankings. In this case, slow and steady wins the race. Blogging is absolutely, positively 100% all about this: it's essentially a vehicle that allows you to easily make regular, useful updates to keep your site both relevant and full of a steady stream of content.

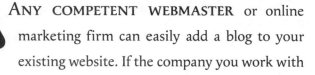

W A R N I N G

ANY COMPETENT WEBMASTER or online marketing firm can easily add a blog to your existing website. If the company you work with tries to charge you more than a couple hundred dollars, tops, to make this change, they are ripping you off.

One question we get regularly at our Technology CLE is "How often should I be blogging? Once a day, once a month?"

To that end, there is a minimum amount of blog posts you should be putting out. Because of Google's preference for updated, steady content, you should be blogging once per week at the very least, equaling 4 blog posts a month. Each blog post should be between about 250 to 800 words; a post can be longer, but it doesn't need to be; it definitely shouldn't be any shorter than 250 words, or Google may mark it down as non-useful.

This may seem daunting to you—and understandably so: the thought of composing another written piece every week isn't appealing to many folks out there. If you truly think about it, however, once a week isn't too bad; that's only four times a month, and if you make a schedule and stick to it, you'll find that blogging really isn't the chore you thought it would be.

> **You must blog consistently to achieve the positive results you're after. If you blog twice one week, skip three weeks and then write four posts the next week, you are not going to see positive results. Google and other search engines only crawl (look at) your website every so often. If they crawl your website and don't see anything new, they move on to your competitors. If they crawl your site and see tons of new content that week, they give you a point for new content, whether the content is one piece or four.**

If you're finding that you have time to write more, it will only benefit you to increase your blog posts to twice a week: that's the optimal number in this situation, and it will most likely net you the most positive credit when Google compiles its local search returns.

Twice a week, however, is plenty: don't go over that! Some people come into this with a very linear mindset. They think that since 2 is better than 1, 5 must be better than 2. It's not... and you'll experience a very diminished rate of return in this regard. 2 blog posts a week is much better than 1, but 5 blog posts a week is barely better than 2. The bottom line is this: if you're spending more than 2 times a week blogging, there are other and probably better things you could be doing with that time!

Interviews From The Field:

Clayton T. Hasbrook - JD
http://www.oklahomalawyer.com/

Is it difficult to balance your time on marketing (blogging, video blasting, content) versus your client work?

Well, it is something that needs to get done. Sometimes, I spend the weekend creating videos or writing blogs to use for marketing. You have to out the effort to get new clients, and marketing is what drives part of your client acquisition.

Is print advertising worth it?

For each client that was coming from the phone books, it was costing $1,200 to acquire each client. We were able to get that number as low as $1,000 per client. We will no longer be doing any print advertising unless there is a large class action suit we need to get involved with.

How do you decide what firms you should use when searching for marketing help?

There is a little sticker shock. You can find web firms that are $2,000 and firms that are over $20,000. That can make it difficult to choose.

What end of the spectrum did you choose?

We went with a company that allowed us flexibility. They are also going to be handling our electronic newsletter.

What other advertising mediums have you worked with?

We have run a few Facebook ads. We have never done any TV ads, and this was something we felt we could control: the time the ad displays, who sees the ad, etc. Our most successful ad was for a medical issue that arose from denture cream. We got a ton of leads from that Facebook ad campaign.

What to Write About:

Having a blog is all well and good, but a blog without useful, relevant content is hardly a blog at all. Here are the three main content points you should be hitting in your blog posts:

1) Talk About What You Do

This one may seem pretty obvious, but it's worth mentioning: talk about what you do, not who you are. Don't talk about yourself, how long your firm's been around or how great your service is: this isn't going to help you at all. You need to fill your blog posts with quality content that relate to the services you do. Quality content is valuable or useful to the user. For example, let's say you're an estate planning attorney involved in VA benefits, and a new law or change happened in VA benefits regulation. A perfect blog post would be a post covering these changes or relevant information pertaining to them. You could title it "Veteran's Assistance benefits: Answers You Need to Know" and formulate it as an easygoing, inside look at how the VA benefits have changed and what that could mean for anyone looking to act on them.

2) Plugged in: Talk About Local Events

#1 on this list may seem obvious to most, but this trick isn't: this is the super-ninja secret of Internet marketing. The trick is this: talk about local events. Blogging about things going on in the community and tying them back into what you do is a fantastic way to make Google and other search engines take notice and gain credit with them in the local search return results. You could, for example, blog about a big event in your city and how it relates to your community. Let's say you live in a college town, and every Saturday during football season, the town quadruples in size. Are you proud of or frustrated by the big event? Do you think it's good or bad for business? Think the traffic isn't worth the amount of money the game brings into the town? Do you have suggestions for parking or must-hit restaurants or activities for the in-bound football fans? A blog post like this will help you with Google because Google will see that you're a part of the community you live in, and (more importantly) it gives Google lots of keyword clues about your location, really helping you to rise to the top in your location.

A simple way to find out what is going on locally is visiting your local news or city website. Find the local events section, click on the story about the event and then curate some content from that post. You can quote several lines from the news source and put those on your blog with your insights about the event and the community. Always be sure to add the URL (website address) of where you found the story. When you add the URL, be sure that it links back to the news website. This will help Google see that you are not only talking about something local to your city but also that the story is being validated by a reputable source.

Additionally, don't feel pressured to make the local blog post about legal issues in the community. In fact, shy away from it. These local community posts are as valuable in their own way as the legal industry posts you make. Someone browsing your website and blogs will have plenty of time to see your other posts and find out about what you do. With a combination of local and legal blogs, you'll get the ranking benefits of all your keyword clues (mentioned above): if someone searches for "VA benefits Dallas, TX" you'll show up because of both your elder law blog posts and your location-based (Dallas, TX), community-based blog posts as well.

Big Tip

You CAN ALWAYS refer to yourself with your keywords!
Don't overdo it, but it's perfectly fine to use things like "As an elder law attorney in Dallas, Texas, I'm always surprised when..." That's the best of both worlds!

Community-based blogs also have the added advantage of making you seem more likeable and down-to-earth, which is always a huge bonus in client interaction. When someone finds your blog and reads through it, it will be beneficial if they get not only practical legal knowledge but also some connection to you as well. When they read your blog, they won't see just another faceless attorney;

they'll read your blog posts about the community and think, "Wow, this person has personality. They seem to really know what they are talking about, AND they are also a part of my community and seem really invested in it."

That person is more likely to pick up the phone and give you a call, and you just got a warm lead by being a personable blogger who talks about the community!

3) Use Other Websites as a Resource

Similar to curating content from a local news organization, you can also find content from other people, news websites or associations that are talking about issues relating to your specific practice area. The best practice for curating content from anther website is to take only a couple of sentences at most and to always link back to the source. It is not good enough to link to the main page of the other website: you should linking directly back to the actual post where you got the information.

If you have friends in other cities that also practice your type of law, you may want to curate some of their content. They will feel special that you took time to link and talk about their blog. In turn, they may do the same for you, building you a stronger overall web presence.

BONUS TIP: *Get other people to write your content for you by asking for guest bloggers. Make sure you always read what p e o p l e write before you post it live to your website. It is your reputation and practice on the line, not theirs, but you shouldn't be afraid of guest posting. Ask people if they would like to submit any articles to your blog, or hold a contest on social media asking people to submit their best posts for your blog and give away prizes. There are lots of places you can find people that are willing to write content for your website; the trick is to ask.*

How to Write:
Be Natural

You don't always have to sound like the smartest person in the world on your blog. This isn't to say you should be sloppy or sound unintelligent, but you shouldn't sound like a king preaching from atop an ivory tower, either. Your clients (and Google) like to see content and blog posts from normal people: conversation, stories and anecdotes are all things they like to index; conversing on your blog makes you more reachable and more indexable.

This isn't just a Google-specific tactic, either; your clients will love you for it as, as mentioned above. It's always been a general marketing strategy to be likeable—it's the age-old marketing concept that people are more likely to work with those similar to themselves.

They see your blog posts and say, "Hey! This person knows what they're talking about and likes what I like." They see a real person with a real family, and it makes them feel more comfortable working with you. A blog is the best place to do this, so plan out your blog structure accordingly. You don't have to do 52 straight weeks of specialty law. Every now and then, you can write an informal "Hey, somebody asked me about this the other day, and I thought I'd talk about it" post.

A good rule of thumb, if you're doing the minimum 4 blogs a month, is to split it up half and half: twice a month goes to business posts, and twice a month goes to local or personal stories. People like to know people: it's a fact of interaction. It will greatly help your sales when prospects feel that they know you more personally. This tactic may feel a little too touchy-feely for some, but don't knock it: it works very well, and blogging is a great way to do it! It drives clients and will improve your ranking, which is, of course, a major goal of this book.

It also helps if you add some images to your blog post. There are lots of places online where you can get royalty free images, which you can use on your website without having to pay anything. Of course, as mentioned in the end of the last chapter, the best thing is to take the images yourself. You will not always be able to take the images on your own camera, so use a combination of both images you find online and your own.

We've had clients that have followed this process to the letter, and their specialty posts about law gained only a few hits and comments. It was their local stories and blog posts, however, that became a focal point; conversations about how bad traffic was when a big event happened got tons of links, comments and opinions from across the board.

In the end, this is what you want: it's the reason for this section and the reason you're branching out into the community. Not only does this sort of activity tied into your locality keywords mean big index boosts from Google (a major goal of this book), it also means very effective general marketing: it makes you a real person that people feel comfortable calling, one of the best advantages you can have in our modern, very skeptical era.

(FIGURE 13)

For a look at some sample blogs, go to the link below. Once you're there, you'll find several blog posts that were written by our staff writers. You can even use these as ideas to start your own blogging. Notice how they were written, why they were written and their use of effective keywords.

To Get the Sample Blogs, go to…

http://www.GetNoticedGetFound.com/sampleblogs

FIGURE 13. BLOG WITH IMAGE

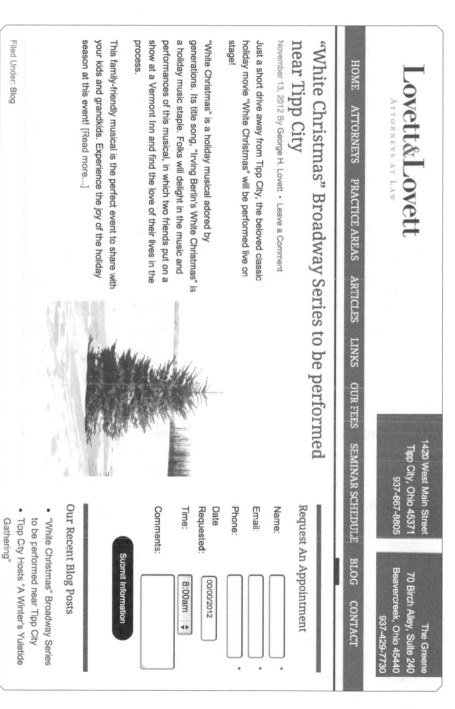

Going Beyond the Blog:
Press Releases

Blogging is not the only way to generate content for your web presence. Press releases are a very powerful tool in getting ranked online and are something you need to be implementing within your overall content strategy. A natural function of press releases is that they will be shared and re-posted all over the Internet. This is one case you are allowed to have duplicate content, including links back to your website.

Because you can have a press release that is syndicated all over the web, you are able to leverage that increase in exposure in the form of back links. Each time you write a press release, you are going to be able to include links to your website. When that press release gets submitted to 20 or more websites, you are creating 20 or back links to your website.

The press releases you write are not for the media, and they are not an attempt at pitching a story to the local news. They are specifically designed to help with your ranking and should be written for Google, not NBC.

PR is also one of the few places where Google expects duplicate content: the more duplicated and shared the press release is, the more important the content must be. This means you can write a press release, put it online and post it to your blog. In fact, we encourage that. Here are some ideas for topics you can write a press release about: (FIGURE 14).

FIGURE 14. GREAT PRESS RELEASE IDEAS

15 Great Press Release Ideas:

1. *Someone in your company is speaking at an industry conference, local chamber, rotary club, etc.*

2. *You hire someone new into your company*

3. *Someone is promoted*

4. *You join an association (local or national)*

5. *You start offering a new service or product*

6. *New office space or additional office added*

7. *Successful client -- create a Case Study and send out press release*

8. *Awards received or recognition from local or national industry or association*

9. *Employee or officers named to charity benefit or non-profit board*

10. *Large sponsor of a charity benefit*

11. *New Business contract awarded*

12. *Having a big promotion or sweepstakes or contest*

13. *Your product and services tie into a big current news item (new government law, health discovery, tax time, new hot-topic movie release, etc.)*

14. *Launch of a new website*

15. *The release of your special report*

What to Do with Your Press Release:

There are both paid and free press sites available. The paid press sites are worth the money because they go out to Associated Press and other big name news wires, like Yahoo and Google News. The more your story gets out there, the greater the possibility (it can happen) that it could get picked up; a local paper could see the press release and pick up the story, for example, and that's a great thing to take advantage of. The problem of duplicate content goes out the window because duplicate content is expected in press releases, and often, the big names, like Associated Press and Reuters, even source duplicate content. The point is that you certainly get what you pay for with press releases. Free submission tools get you as much as you paid for them—zero.

For a FREE listing of the press release websites we currently use to syndicate content, go to the site below. Once there, you'll also find a few press release examples (ones we have used in the past). That way, you'll have some great ideas on how to start writing.

To Get the Press Releases and Press Sites we use, go to...

www.GetNoticedGetFound.com/pressreleases

The Structure of a Press Release:

There is a certain way you are supposed to write a press release, and there are some rules you have to follow. Press releases are designed to disseminate information or notices of what's going on in the world. This is not a platform to talk about how awesome you are or to pitch your services. Not that you shouldn't be broadcasting your firm in a positive manner, just keep the sales pitch to a minimum.

Here is the basic structure of a press release: (FIGURE 15)

As mentioned in the introduction to press releases, you are able to get a lot of links back to your website. What you put into the body of the press release does not need to be earth-shattering news. While you are writing this press release, you will need to make sure you add some links in order to make your press release effective. The best place to add links is in the body, in the conclusion and in the boilerplate.

Most press release companies that you submit your press release to will usually allow up to three places where you can add links. The links you should add include one to your home page, your blog and possibly a video or subpage on your website (for example, attorney profile page or contact page).

Don't be shocked if you write a press release and get an email back from the company stating that your press release has been rejected. This can happen the first time you start writing press releases if the content of the press release does not match what they deem newsworthy. Usually, this occurs when a press release sounds too much like a sales pitch. Go back, make your edits and try again.

FIGURE 15. SAMPLE PRESS RELEASE

[Firm Logo]

Contact: Joe Smith
Tel: 555-555-5555
Email: Joe@SmithandSmith.com
FOR IMMEDIATE RELEASE

MAIN TITLE OF PRESS RELEASE GOES IN ALL
UPPER CASE AND SHOULD BE CENTERED

Subtitle Is Also Centered and Should Be Upper and Lower Case

This is the summary body of the press release. It should be a short paragraph that outlines what the news concerns and why it is important.

This is the body of the press release. Include quotes from people, who can be people at your firm or people that were quoted in other media outlets on the specific nature of your press release. This is the body of the press release. Include quotes from people, who can be people at your firm or people that were quoted in other media outlets on the specific nature of your press release.

This is the body of the press release. Include quotes from people, who can be people at your firm or people that were quoted in other media outlets on the specific nature of your press release. This is the body of the press release. Include quotes from people, who can be people at your firm or people that were quoted in other media outlets on the specific nature of your press release.

The concluding statement or wrap goes here and should be no more than one or two sentences. The concluding statement or wrap goes here and should be no more than one or two sentences.

Your boilerplate (or who you are) goes here. Your boilerplate (or who you are) goes here. Your boilerplate (or who you are) goes here. Your boilerplate (or who you are) goes here.

#####

If you'd like more information about this topic or to schedule a media appearance with Joe Smith, please call Jane Doe at 555-555-5555 or email Jane@smithandsmith.com.

Interviews From The Field:

Interview with Scott Mozarsky, Chief Commercial Officer, PR Newswire

You know a lot about law firm marketing—tell us your background?

I started as an attorney in '93. Back then, the world was clearly a different world, and a lot of law firms didn't even have email accounts. Attorneys were still reliant on faxing to send information. One observation back then is that marketing was a taboo subject, and if it was marketing, it was taking out a huge advertisement in American Lawyer Magazine. There weren't legal events you went to for marketing; there weren't Linkedin groups for attorneys. I watched this evolve. It was really a transformation and change in the media industry.

So, what has changed with regard to PR?

Back in the day, the news release was a way to get into a paper; that is what it was for. For me, back in the day, you used our services to put out a press release if you wanted someone to write an article about it. Well, the world has changed. The value prop-osition is less about getting the newsrooms and newspapers to write about you; it's about getting visibility online.

Attorneys haven't done a great job of reaching the larger percent-age of their audience with their content. One of the things a wire service [PR] can be used for is to amplify your efforts. They used to use the wire to announce major events, and now, they can drive traffic to their website through frequent content dissemination. This gets people to use your firm's website to learn and engage in issues.

It's also about engagement. We are in the age of big data, and we have more and more visibility of who is viewing our content and how. This can be used to nurture the people that are engaging with your content and bring them in.

The use of social media and video is also important. Lots of law firms are nervous about using social [media] because they are afraid of giving up control. As long as you have social media pol-icies in place, you can regain some of that control. Your social image is important; people are doing Google searches about you. When someone meets an attorney, they are doing a Google and Linkedin search to learn about the person.

How can a law firm use the press or content to grow their practice?

The best way to drive growth is to put out compelling content that your audience wants to engage with. Rather, it is blogs, videos or photos. Then, listen to what they are saying, and target where the best conversations are going. Then, engage in those conversations. Establish yourself as a thought leader, and drive more and more reputational gain and ultimately more business that way.

What are some examples of how law firms could use press releases?

Let's say there is a law firm that blogs on a certain topic. Maybe they specialize in securities law. When someone at the firm is blogging on regulatory developments impacting securities law or on a key issue like disclosure of regulation, the wire is a great way to get that information out. What we've found is the use of our online network may not be to get into a newspaper, but to:

A) Get the release seen by a number of people on our network.

B) Get that information downstream to a number of other sites and relevant blogs that might carry it. That's effectively syndication.

C) Have the ability for it [the press release] to show up high in organic search because Google treats

us as a publisher. Generally, our stuff does show
up on the first page in organic search.

That's a powerful way to have your content show up on the first
page of search and drive a lot of traffic to your blog. There is an
audience out there that is looking for that information.

Or, if there is a court ruling or regulatory change with respect to
tort reform, for instance, a great opportunity for law firms doing
personal injury is to go out and speak to the issue. Use that issue
as a platform to better engage with the users out there and target
them as potential clients.

It's not about a newspaper article; it is about getting your information online.

> *Press Releases are displayed online*
> *in certain unique areas of websites.*
> *Does where wire content ends up*
> *make a difference?*

Yes. Because the content is value driven, it ends up in the main
content area of websites. You end up in a sweet [middle] spot
around earned media [ads]. This enables law firms to engage in
marketing without the stigma, right? Back in the day, when law
firms [felt that they] shouldn't be engaging in a lot of marketing,
it needed to be word of mouth. Now, with earned media, you

provide constituents, people you want to reach, with something of value. Rather, it's a whitepaper, a three-minute video talking about a subject, infographics, webinars, whatever it is, you are providing valuable content. In return, the quid pro quo is you're going to get feedback from your constituents, you are going to get data from them and you are going to better able to engage with them. When you engage, you will be able to form a stronger relationship with them.

What things should attorneys be careful of with regard to press releases?

There are clearly issues of bumping up against regulation, areas where you could hurt your credibility. Any content a law firm is putting out on a wire should be less about marketing and more educational. Your content should deliver value to the constituents out there. What this does is establish a level of credibility to the firm because it doesn't look like they are just out there trying to drive business.

When I think about the regulatory issues, when a firm has a specialty, clearly there are regulations that don't allow advertising in connection with a product up for FDA approval.

Law firms should also refrain from giving legal advice [in press releases]. A firm cannot go out and make statements that are unsubstantiated to try and sway public opinion on something.

We use your services for our clients and have been very happy. In your own words, why should law firms consider using PR Newswire?

Offline, we have the broadest and deepest distribution network in the world. We have 50,000 clients, ranging from a one-person company in the garage all the way up to Microsoft and IBM. As far as online, our online statics Google page ranks best in the industry, inbound links best in the industry, traffic by our website best in the industry. We also have a great set of tools. Our global spread is unmatched.

Why you should use a content distribution service is the real question. If you are a smaller or mid-size firm, you can level the playing field. Rather than put a banner ad in a local newspaper, what you really want to be able to do is get in front of the person that is doing a web search for your expertise. Or, get in front of the person looking for a blog. Then, you get your name in front of them in hopes that they come back to you. Before, the largest firms had the advantage because ads are expensive. Now, any firm can get their content out online.

Videos:
How YouTube Changed Video and What This Means for Your Firm

Something great happened in the world of video production: this little company came along that allowed people to upload their own videos. Couple this new service with advancements in general consumer video equipment, and you had a perfect storm for an industry-changing event: video no longer needs to cost $30,000 to produce.

What this means for your firm is that you are able to produce your own videos, or pay a nominal fee, and create tons of content. You still need to maintain a professional image in your videos, just like your website should reflect your actual office in its professional appearance, but you are going to be able to get the professional quality you need for next to nothing.

There are two kinds of videos you should be focusing on, with an accompanying strategy on how to use those videos. The first type of video you should have is something for the home page of your website. This video should be about 90 seconds long and should (but doesn't have to) have someone from your firm on the video. We help our clients do this and, for some clients, actually fly out and do the production to create their home page videos. Here is the structure that you should follow (hint, this is the exact structure of our videos that we produce):

Intro: My name is Joe Smith, and I am a senior attorney here at Smith and Smith.

Lead In: Thank you for taking the time to visit our website.

Body: We understand that your situation can be stressful and difficult to understand. Since each person is unique, we take pride in getting to know our clients' specific needs and circumstances. The reason we got into practicing this kind of law is _____. We are really connected to our community by _____ and would love for you to visit our office.

Conclusion: Since we are sure you have a few questions, please feel free to read our blog, schedule an appointment or sign up for our special report, where you can learn more about hiring a YOUR FIRM_____attorney.

This is a basic, brief script for a video that should appear on your home page. When producing this video, think about speaking directly to a prospect's needs. We typically produce the video in our client's office, often with them sitting down, and include a graphic on the bottom of the video with the client's full name and firm name. You do not need to add any graphics at the end with your website URL or contact information. The person watching is most likely already on your website; if they are watching this video on YouTube, then you will have your URL and information in the description below the video.

For an example of a video, please visit the link below. You are free to follow the script on the video and send the video to your production person as an example of what you would like to have produced.

www.GetNoticedGetFound.com/samplevideo

The next kind of video you will need is content-specific video. Mike Koenigs, a good friend of ours and the founder of Traffic Geyser and Instant Customer, has an ingenious technique for creating video content quickly and easily.

The concept is simple: create 20 videos, each less than 2 minutes in length. To create the content on the video, write out 10 questions you are frequently asked by your clients (and/or prospects) and 10 questions that people should ask you but don't.

Then, have someone sit off camera and ask you the questions. Repeat the question, then answer it. Here is a simple example:

Off Camera: "How often should an attorney blog?"

On Camera: "I often get asked by attorneys, 'How often I should blog?' This is something that plagues attorneys when they are developing their online marketing strategy. The answer is actually simple: about 4 times a month. We strongly recommend once a week as Google likes to see consistency..."

OR

Off Camera: "Should attorneys blog about local events?"

On Camera: "A question that I do not often get asked, but I should, is whether or not attorneys should blog about local events happening in their communities and city. The answer is a resounding YES, they should. Attorneys should be blogging about local events at least once or twice a month. The easiest way to..."

You get the idea. Using this method of question and answer will produce a very easy-to-watch video. It is also easy to record these types of videos because you are talking about topics you know inside and out, things you tell your new clients regularly and questions you get asked all the time.

Once you have recorded these 20 videos, have your video person chop them into individual video clips. Add a graphic page on the end directing people back to your blog. It is a great soft sell to send someone to your blog. It says, "I'm not going to push you into making this decision, so please come read some more information."

On your videos, never say things like "If you want to hire me" or "To work with our firm." Meeting a prospect on the Internet and then having them transform into a real paying client is a lot like getting into a relationship: you have to hold hands before you kiss, and you should go on a couple of dates before you get married.

Where to Post Videos:

Video content should go several places. The first place is, of course, your website. We recommend that you upload a video from your 20 content videos to your blog every other week. (This does not count as your weekly blog post.) The easiest way to add the video to your blog is to upload the video to YouTube first.

When you are uploading a video to YouTube or any other website, the description is very important. This is your opportunity to tell the search engines what this video is about. Make sure to add your keywords, location and URL in a natural way.

Here is an example: (FIGURE 16)

As a Seattle Divorce Attorney, Mike Fancher discusses the difference between pre-nuptials and post-nuptials and how those can influence your decisions when getting divorced. For more information, please visit our blog http:///url.com/Blog

When adding a link to your video description, you must add the http:// before the www. This ensures that your URL will be a clickable link and not something the user will have to copy and paste.

Once you've posted your video online, it's time to syndicate it, aka blast it all over the web. There are about 25 video-hosting websites on which you should have accounts. For our clients, we prefer to blast to every video hosting website. These sites are all free and include Vimeo, Metacafe and even YouTube. For a complete list of these sites, Google "Post my video online."

Sometimes, you are even able to embed a video inside your press release. Not every press release or blog post needs a video, but it occasionally helps provide another layer to your content and improves your overall content reach. People love watching videos, and the search engines love seeing video content on websites.

FIGURE 16 . FANCHERS VIDEO

How to Manage Multiple Locations:
Content, Websites, and Directory Listings

Many firms we work with have more than one location, which leads to a lot of questions about how to handle content, videos, website and local directory listings. There is more wrong advice out there about this exact topic than almost any other search-related issue.

The first step to managing multiple locations is to create a strategy outlining what your expected results are for each location. If you have one office that is your main location and three smaller satellite offices, this will impact the strategy you take with regard to your web presence. The great news is there are a few things that remain the same regardless of the number of locations you may have:

1. All your locations should appear under one website. There was a point in time when the search engines didn't care if you had one website with every location or multiple websites with one location on each. That has changed over the last year, and Google has made it very clear that one website is preferred.

2. Each location will need to be optimized within your content strategy. This means that you will need to blog, create videos and submit press releases that highlight each location separately. Since we recommend about 1 – 2 pieces of local content each month, your blog will need to have 1 -2 pieces per location if you want them all to rank at the top of the list. This is where planning is important. If you have an office that does not generate much business, but you still meet clients there and thus need that location's information on your website, you may be inclined to spend very little time optimizing for that

location. So, proper planning is important—and you can always focus on one location first, then add the other locations into your content strategy at a later time.

3. Your different locations still need to appear on the home page. This can be tricky, especially for firms with more than three locations. This is where really good design work and someone with expertise in usability (designing the layout of websites to optimize for the user experience) is crucial. A professional designer should be able to give you a couple of options for displaying multiple locations on the home page in a professional manner. If you have more than 10 offices, you will have to get creative. Try designing a site that has dynamic navigation – this is a fancy way of saying a navigation bar that changes as you move your mouse around the website.

Contact Pages:

For each location, you should create a separate page with that location's specific information, a Google map and address. You will also want to have a contact page that includes every location on the same page. On the contact page that has every firm's location, avoid putting full maps on this page. It tends to look sloppy and can be very confusing when trying to navigate around the page. Since you set up a page for each location, just link from your main contact page to the sub-location page. Doing this also provides a nice SEO boost to each address because the search engines will see a dedicated page signaling that location.

ON EACH LOCATION'S subpage there are three areas where you must pay special attention: the title tag, category and microfor- matting. Each location's subpage should have the city and state in the title tag of that page. That page then needs to have a microformat that contains that location's specific city and state. Then, to help the search engines out, you should create a separate category for each page that also contains the city and state.

Directory Listings:

In chapter 8, we completely cover properly establishing directory listings. In this brief section, we wanted you to see what extra steps are required when you have multiple locations. Please reference chapter 8 for questions about setting up directory listings.

There are a few things you need to consider when managing multiple locations and properly creating your citations (online directory listings). Generally, you should never have multiple Google Plus Local (Google+ Local) pages; however that only applies when you have a single location. When you have multiple locations, here is what you should keep in mind:

1. **Create a Separate Directory Listing for Each Location**

Each location should have its own set of directory listings. On Google+ Local, Yelp and at least 15 of the other top directory listing websites, your individual locations need their own directory listings. You can set up these directory listings with your firm's name, the location's phone number and the same description as your main location. When you go to enter your location's URL (website), make sure that you are linking to that location's specific webpage on your website. This is what that link should look like: http://www.YourLawFirm.com/contact/city_state

2. **Directory Listings May Vary by City**

What is fascinating about local directory listings is that each city has its own unique twist. Recently, GetListed.org, managed by David Mihm, collaborated with WhiteSpark.ca (http://www.WhiteSpark.ca), managed by Darren Shaw, to find out if there is any discrepancy from one city to the next with regard to which directory service should be focused on. Should you only focus on the major sites, like Yelp and Google, or could there be other websites that locals are using to find businesses? As it turns out, there are local website that rank as high and sometimes higher than the major directory listing sites. For example, in Santa Barbara, CA, the website http://www.santabarbara.com ranks higher than Yelp. This is incredibly valuable information, and you can find more out about the study here: http://getlisted.org/resources/local-citations-by-city.aspx. What this means for your firm is that you need to do separate research for each location to determine what sites rank the best. Once you compile a list of the top sites, you can ensure that your firm has a directory listing on each of them. To figure this out, all you need to do is Google a common phrase like "best dentist in Topeka, KS," then "Oil Change Topeka, KS" and finally "Your Type of Law Topeka, KS". Then, compare all the results. Is there a website that is ranking higher than the major websites for each search? If so, there is an additional directory listing you will need to create.

3.   Geo-Location Photos

If you are uploading geo-tagged photos to your Panoramio account, you should be linking to those images in each location's individual directory listing. This last technique is not required for most law firms, unless you are in a more competitive market like personal injury or DUI. This also only works if your camera has the ability to geo-tag photos with imbedded coordinates. or if you or your webmaster manually add the geo-tags to the photos using a geo-tagging service, such as Panoramio or Picasa.

- Blogs, press releases, videos and social media content are the best methods for creating regularly-updated, quality content, which is ESSENTIAL to get ranked highly on Google.

- YOU HAVE TO HAVE A BLOG, it must be on your website and it should be updated at least once a week. Your blog should talk about topics related to your services, current legal news and community events or local news—in a natural and readable way.

- A blog will work wonders for your website: it shows Google that you have current, relevant legal and local content (which will improve your ranking), and it shows potential clients that you are knowledgeable about your field of law as well as an active, likeable member of your community.

- Press releases are very effective because they are syndicated all over the web, adding tons of back links to your website.

- Press releases are the one place where Google expects duplicate content—the more the release is syndicated and duplicated, the more important it must be, so also post it to your blog!

- Press releases must follow certain guidelines for content (must be news-worthy, e.g. an attorney just joined a bar association), voice (no overt advertising language), and structure.

- Video is HUGE online—both people and Google love video content—and it may cost less to create than you'd expect. Video should go on your website and be syndicated all over the web.

- Add a video to the home page of your website that features an attorney in your office and speaks to a potential client's needs.

- Create video "snippets" that are content-specific—answering the questions that a potential client might be wondering about their legal problem or your firm—and syndicate these.

Notes

CHAPTER 7

What?!?! I Have to Use Social Media?!

Using Facebook, Twitter, g+, LinkedIn and the Rest

W e know some of you are snickering. We know some of you are sitting in your home or office, having read the title of this particular chapter, and are thinking "Twitter! That can't possibly help me."

We know how silly Twitter sounds. We know the derision it's received from all sides, including our friends and the media. But don't laugh just yet. The fact of the matter is that Twitter is relevant. As much as it pains us to say this, Twitter may be one of the more important factors that figures into your Internet marketing strategy.

So, you better get tweeting!

We are going to cover what social media means to your local rankings, why it matters and what you should be focusing on. You will be pleasantly surprised with the information we have and our instructions for you. This is one area where you need to check specifically with your bar association to ensure that you are 100% informed about your state regulations, as they may differ from this chapter's information.

Why Social Media?

Simply put, social media is starting to become a very powerful force in how Google is determining what is relevant online. The Internet is full of bots, scammers, article spinners and links to irrelevant or otherwise spammy articles. Social media, however, does the vetting by itself. Users of social media sites aren't going to share spammy links with each other; they're going to share real content. As a result, Google has realized that indexing and calculating relevancy from social media is very beneficial since social media (in general) has real people posting real content: content that was valuable enough to warrant a "Hey, check this out" from one person to another.

Some of us have been trying to avoid social media for one reason or the other: privacy, general lack of interest or whatever other reasons you may have avoided it thus far. The statistics on social media and Internet marketing, however, can't be denied:

- Facebook, as of this writing, has over nine hundred million users. To put that into perspective, that means Facebook has about three times as many users as the

U.S. population; this is very important in terms of saturation.

- Twitter boasts that it has broken the barrier of 200 million tweets in one day.

- Pinterest and Google+ both reached 10 million users in less than 6 months.

What these statistics should show you is that social media is an extremely influential force in today's cultural mindset, and it's only getting stronger. Social media is here to stay: more and more people are joining every day and getting recommendations from their friends and family about great services that they received.

Google has been taking notice of this and responding accordingly and so should you. In this chapter, we're going to take a look at social networks and your strategy for them: we're going to figure out just how to approach these social media websites and use them to help Google notice you!

The Social Networks

In the social media game, there are currently several huge players, but we are going to focus on Facebook, Twitter, Google+ and LinkedIn. This isn't to say you should ignore the other social media networks out there; they're still important and, in fact, location-based social media like Foursquare and Facebook Places are very useful too. You may want to have a presence in those as well as other minor social networks, such as Pinterest, Klout, Quora, etc.

For the core of your marketing strategy, however, we're going to focus on the big four. This focus will give you the most coverage and best ROI in terms of time spent on marketing, so it's how we'll proceed!

Interviews From The Field:

Beth Noble — JD
Leone Noble Seate

www.defendmyrightsnow.com

Social media is fairly new in general. What are the ways you are using social media with your firm, and what are the results you have seen?

At first, I was very skeptical of social media and even our web presence because I knew our clients, and I was sure they were not looking for an attorney online. After doing some research, I found that over 80% of households had high-speed Internet access in my town.

That made me rethink if I should be getting online with my marketing. Of course, I was reluctant to get into social media. Why would someone care if I am on Twitter? After meeting with someone that does a lot of online marketing, I decided to give social media a try. After 1 month, we saw our website traffic double, and it has increased every month since then!

Have you seen any results from social media?

We knew that if we increase our traffic to our website we would increase our business. It is not generally the case that we get clients directly from Twitter or Facebook, but we are getting more clients because our traffic is up.

How are you managing your online marketing?

This has actually become a full-time job for me at my firm. I was a trial lawyer and loved it. Now, I have found that I really enjoy the marketing side of the business as well, even more than the practicing of law. What works with our firm is that I have partners that are willing to let me stop generating fees and start working to bring the cases into the firm. If I had to practice law at my firm, I would have no choice but to hire someone to do the marketing for us.

What are you doing to boost your online presence?

We blog. I put at least one new piece of content on my website each week and we send our articles to syndication sites like e-zine as well. It is important to get your content out and to get back links to your website as well.

Where did you learn all this?

I am self-taught. I spent hours and hours reading, going online, hiring marketing firms and understanding the basics of online marketing. I even bought a book on Wordpress to understand better how our website works. This is something I love and find fascinating.

Facebook

Facebook is the biggest social media site in the room, the 800-pound gorilla: everybody knows and uses it, so you're going to need to capitalize on that. The first thing you should have is a fan page, so we'll take a look at how to create one and how to link it into your overall Internet marketing strategy.

MANY OF YOU will be scared of Facebook's privacy implications. It's very important to note that your business page is NOT your personal page. It's not connected to your personal page, it's not the same thing as your personal page, and nothing you post on your personal page will appear on your business page and vice versa. They are completely separate entities! For those of you resisting joining Facebook or afraid your fan page will expose your personal page, fear not: none of your personal information will go on your fan page, and your privacy is safe.

Your Facebook Page

A page, quite simply, represents your business. There are two reasons you need a Facebook page: for the link back to your website and because people may expect you to have one. This is important information because it will shape your overall Facebook strategy. You can use Facebook to grow a fan base, increase your brand awareness and get new clients. When it comes to local search ranking and spending your time wisely, it is recommended that you do not put a ton of energy into building a Facebook dynasty. Instead, use Facebook as a linking location and a reputation guardian.

Facebook can be a very organic way of getting warm leads and targeted marketing. Facebook users are already in the social media world, surfing around, and in their social network traversal, they may stumble on your page and think, "Wow! I might need a lawyer for setting up my upcoming adoption plans." (In fact, the #1 demographic of Facebook is 25-34 and 35-54 year old females.) Source: http://mashable.com/2012/03/09/social-media-demographics/

This is a massive, growing target market of the many people who need attorneys for all kinds of reasons: divorce, personal injury, estate planning, etc. It definitely has the right mix of people with the money and motive to hire attorneys, and your page on Facebook will be a great place for them to get in touch with you regarding their problems.

Setting up a Facebook page is simple and only takes about 10 minutes (since you already have your website up and running, the information is all in one place).

1. Log into Facebook http://www.facebook.com/pages/create.php and select local business.

2. Add your business information, including your real address and the actual phone number to your office (no tracking numbers allowed).

3. Set up an account. You have two options here: either log in as you (again, your personal information will not be used on your page; this is just to ensure you are a real person, not a scamming computer program) or create a new account.

4. Add an image. In this step, you should choose "Import image from web" and select an image from your website that is also geo-located.

5. Add "About Me" information and the URL to your website. It automatically provides the http:// which you want to keep. You can add multiple websites here. We recommend adding your home page, blog and YouTube channel.

6. Your page is live—now, complete as much as you can. There are options to add more images, a banner image called a "cover photo" and post a status update. Complete any other areas you can.

Here is what that process looks like with screenshots walking you though step by step. (FIGURE 17)

FIGURE 17. FACEBOOK SCREENSHOTS
(STEP 1-6)

facebook

Create a Facebook Account

I already have a Facebook account

Email:

New Password: [?]

Date of Birth: Month: ◆ Day: ◆ Year: ◆
Please enter your own date of birth. Why is this required?

Security Check:

Enter both words below, separated by a space.
Can't read the words below? Try different words or an audio captcha.

himself

Text in the box: What's this?

☐ I have read and agree to the Terms of Use and Privacy Policy

Sign Up Now!

Problems signing up? Check out our help pages

Facebook © 2012 · English (US)   Mobile · Find Friends · Badges · People · Pages · Apps · Games · Music · About · Create an Ad · Create a Page · Developers · Careers · Privacy · Cookies · Terms · Help

---

facebook   Settings   Logout

Set Up Clark & Lord, Attorneys at Law

1 Profile Picture   2 About   3 Enable Ads

Upload From Computer | Import From Website

Save Photo **Skip**

Facebook © 2012 · English (US)   About · Create an Ad · Create a Page · Developers · Careers · Privacy · Cookies · Terms · Help

---

facebook   Settings   Logout

Set Up Clark & Lord, Attorneys at Law

1 Profile Picture   **2 About**   3 Enable Ads

Tip: Add a description and website to improve the ranking of your page in search.

Clark & Lord is a full-service law firm protecting clients' interests in the fields of family law (divorce, paternity, support, marital settlement agreements, custody), criminal defense (felony, misdemeanor, DUI, and infractions), and juvenile work.

http://clarkandlordlaw.com/   Remove

http://clarkandlordlaw.com/blog/   Add Another Site

Will this Page represent a real establishment, business or venue? [?] ⦿ Yes ◯ No

Visit Help Center   **Save Info** **Skip**

Facebook © 2012 · English (US)   About · Create an Ad · Create a Page · Developers · Careers · Privacy · Cookies · Terms · Help

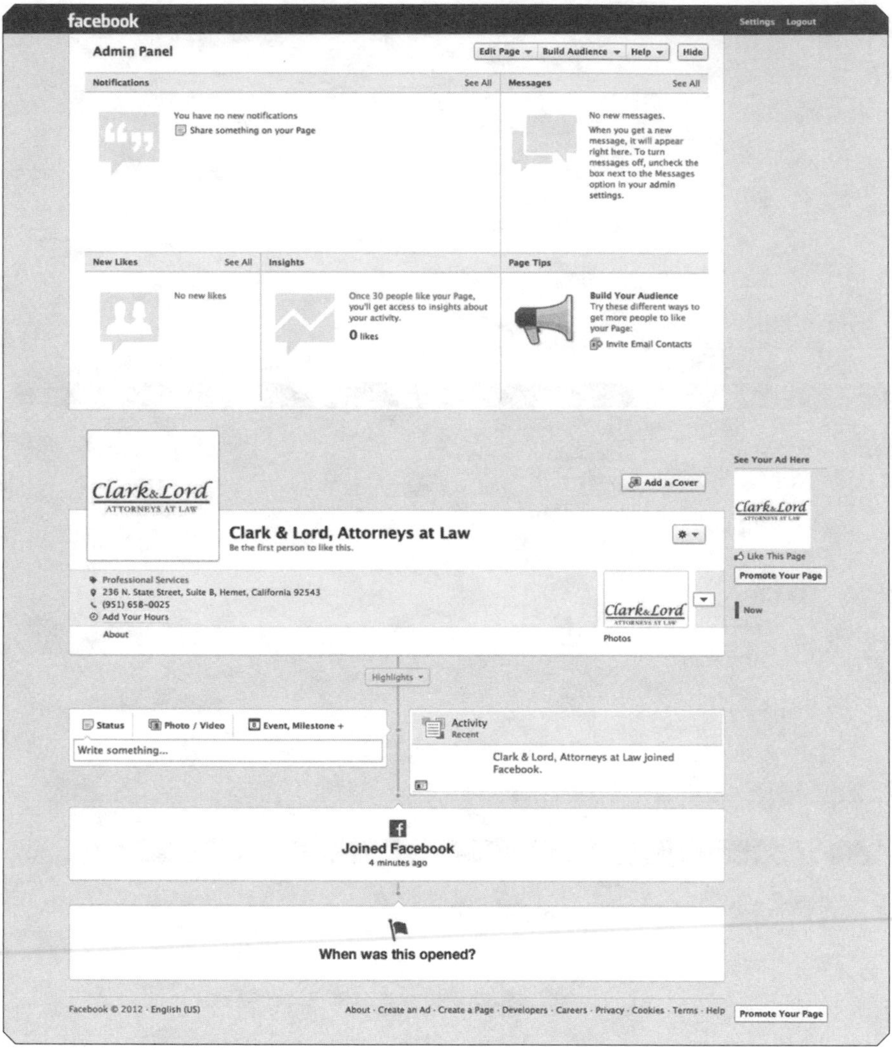
facebook
Settings Logout
Admin Panel
Edit Page
Build Audience
Help
Hide
Notifications
See All
You have no new notifications
Share something on your Page
Messages
See All
No new messages.
When you get a new message, it will appear right here. To turn messages off, uncheck the box next to the Messages option in your admin settings.
New Likes
See All
No new likes
Insights
Once 30 people like your Page, you'll get access to insights about your activity.
0 likes
Page Tips
Build Your Audience
Try these different ways to get more people to like your Page:
Invite Email Contacts
Clark & Lord
ATTORNEYS AT LAW
Add a Cover
Clark & Lord, Attorneys at Law
Be the first person to like this.
Professional Services
236 N. State Street, Suite B, Hemet, California 92543
(951) 658-0025
Add Your Hours
About
Photos
See Your Ad Here
Like This Page
Promote Your Page
Now
Highlights
Status
Photo / Video
Event, Milestone +
Write something...
Activity
Recent
Clark & Lord, Attorneys at Law joined Facebook.
Joined Facebook
4 minutes ago
When was this opened?
Facebook © 2012 · English (US)
About · Create an Ad · Create a Page · Developers · Careers · Privacy · Cookies · Terms · Help
Promote Your Page

While you're creating your Facebook page, don't forget about your Facebook Places page as well. The location-based aspect of this is really attractive, especially because of the proliferation of mobile phones. More and more people are buying smartphones and more and more things are going mobile. (We'll talk more about this in the Mobile chapter.) With a Places page, people checking in on their mobile phone to see what's around them can find your business. You can also offer specials through this mode of delivery. At the very least, create these pages, but you can take it further and be creative. Combine things like your fan page and places page, and figure out ways to synergize the two to make an effective marketing vehicle.

What to Do with Your New Page:

The main focus of your page is the linking, which you have 50 percent complete because you added your URL to the About Me section. Now, you need to post a status update with the link to your blog post each time you write a blog.

Don't worry about updating your status on Facebook with what coffee you drank that morning or how hungry you are for lunch. All we are concerned with here is creating a link on your page back to your blog post.

This is perhaps the most important thing to know about social media in general: all of these pages can be linked together in different ways. There are so many options for managing business pages and Places pages that it's vital you have a professional who knows how to set up social media correctly. Barring that, you need to get online and do some extensive research into establishing the proper social media channels: it's not something you can just cobble together quickly.

Once you've got your business and Places pages set up, it's time to move on!

Twitter

Twitter is one of the more active social networks out there and perhaps one that inspires the most reluctance to join. The media and our peers have vilified it, but the fact remains that Twitter is important.

In fact, this is the whole reason Twitter is so important: every single tweet (a "tweet" is what each individual Twitter post is called) is indexed by Google and able to be seen by every search engine. Some social networks, like Facebook and occasionally LinkedIn, need a username and password to see most of their content; with Twitter, there's no requirement to log in to see individual tweets. What this means is that Google can index all the tweets out there and that Twitter informs Google page rankings enormously: Google uses people's tweets to help gauge the importance of pages all around the Internet. These are called social signals. Pages and websites with lots of links from Twitter are going to increase in importance: you don't want to be spammy, but you do want to take advantage of this fact.

That's the basis of most of your Twitter interaction, when it's all said and done: taking advantage of Twitter's ability to generate constant content without coming across as being spammy. You can't just blast out links to your blog articles all day in a stream of useless or irrelevant content from you (or rehashed content). This isn't going to help you to increase your page rank.

Here is some terminology you should know about Twitter:

- Posts on Twitter are called "Tweets"
- Re-posting something is called "Re-Tweeting"
- You "Follow" people, and people that follow you are called "Followers"
- DM stands for "Direct Message," which is a private (non-public) message to another Twitter user (something a senator from New York thought he was doing, but he accidently sent it publically instead).
- Hashtags (#) are used to anchor a tweet to a topic. For example: New blog post on #Law #Marketing about social media at http://www.gngf....
- The @ symbol is how you mention someone else in a tweet and also acts as the reply function if you are trying to reply to a tweet someone posted.

Much like the techniques described in the Going Local chapter, you'll to want to create a bunch of tweets about local events as well as topical content, like minor changes in law—changes that would be important or useful for people to know. Your tweets are going to be composed of content similar to your blogs, just shortened down to the 140 character limit per tweet and sent out once or twice a day.

This may seem as daunting as the blogging, especially considering the daily frequency of the tweets. Truth be told, however, 140 characters is not that much at all. You don't have to sit by the computer and send them out one by one; there are tons of websites and programs that let you schedule tweets, including HootSuite (http://hootsuite.com), SocialOomph (http://www.socialoomph.com) and more. You can sit down for an hour and write enough tweets for a week or two, schedule them and forget about them until the next week, when you sit down to write some more.

Note: Setting up services that automate your social media posts is a quick and easy way to save time, but there is a cost to convenience: posts submitted by these services get less weight with Google and other search engines. For the best and biggest bang for your buck, posting from the actual sites, like Twitter and Facebook, are recommended.

(FIGURE 18)

Don't be tempted to tweet an exact duplicate of content from your blog posts or articles! Your tweets should be on the same topic as your blog posts, but they shouldn't be copied and pasted straight from the blog. What you can do, however, is link back to your blog from your tweets; in fact, this is not only permissible but also encouraged. There are plugins available for countless blogging platforms that enable you to automatically send out a tweet with a link to your blog post every time you create a new blog post. Take advantage of that to generate links to your blog posts that aren't spammy (since they're only once or twice a week). It's a great tool for slowly and steadily creating links back to your blog. There are also plugins for Facebook as well. Make sure that each time you post a blog, it's at least getting automatically posted to your Twitter and Facebook page, if not posted manually.

The next layer of Twitter—and the strength of this social network—is getting people to favorite and share your information. The Re-Tweet tells the search engines that not only is the information you shared relevant to you, your audience gives it an endorsement. This would be just like a person sending out an email endorsing your

Figure 18. Image For Twitter

latest move into a new area of law. That is far more powerful than you just saying it.

In order to get people to Re-Tweet your posts, you'll need people to follow you. This is actually really easy on Twitter. Type into the search box on Twitter keyword(s) specific to your type of law, for example: Adoption Attorney.

(Figure 19)

Twitter will return two types of returns: tweets and people that are connected to that phrase. Select the option to view the people connected with that phrase, and start following people. It is perfectly acceptable on Twitter to follow complete strangers. Twitter makes

Figure 19. Twitter Search Box

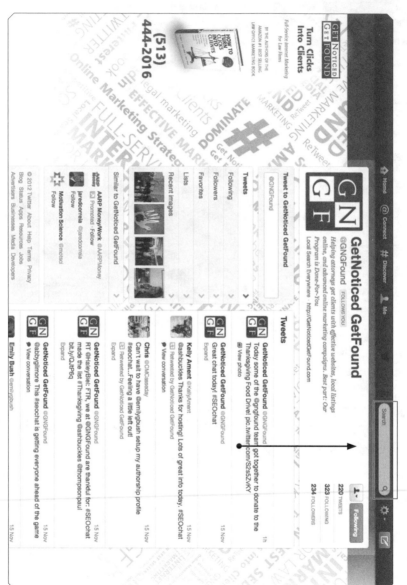

this really simple: with one click of the button, you can "Follow" someone. Go down the list and start with adding the first 50 people.

Then, type in another keyword(s), and select the first 50 people. You are limited, an attempt to avoid scammers, from adding more than 100 people in a day.

So, how do you get people to follow you?

The two best techniques are interaction with the people you are following and re-tweeting your followers' tweets. If you log into Twitter to make your post, re-tweet one tweet from someone you are following and reply to one tweet with either a "good point" or "interesting article you posted," you will be on the road to building a following.

Start slow—don't spend too much time on it, and think about Twitter as something you can do a little tiny bit every day. In two years, you'll have a formidable Twitter presence. Remember to post your own blog posts as links once or twice a week and, other than that, tweet about anything you feel would be interesting to your audience—from news stories to comments about law.

Google+
and How It Is Different from Facebook, LinkedIn, YouTube and Twitter

This is not Google's first attempt at social media. Understanding how these sites are all different and how they operate helps explain Google+ (g+). The other important piece to this social and search puzzle is the recent merger of Google Places with g+ to create Google+ Local. Now, g+Local replaces Google Places. We will specifically cover your g+Local page later; for now, let's dig into g+ and how it works as a social media network.

Here are the four major social networks and what their functions are:

YouTube – I make a video. You search for it and can watch, share or comment on my video. As a search based network, this is the most open network of them all. Few people use the subscribe function as a social element.

LinkedIn – Used to be: Here is my resume. Please higher me — Now is: I need a job; I collaborate with my colleagues & vendors to learn and grow in groups and I get / answer questions. The most closed network of the 4: you must know my email, already have worked with me or be in a group with me to connect.

Twitter – I can push information out to many people, and this information can be spread quickly. Google indexes this network, which is a bonus. As many people as are on Twitter can follow my updates. You can follow me, and I do not need to follow you. Information is sent out in short bursts, and interaction takes place both on Twitter (in a short conversation style) and off Twitter (follow this link to see this video, read my blog, etc).

Facebook – The current king of social media. Facebook is about "friendships." You and I must mutually know and/or like each other to share information. I can post information in the hopes that this information is seen on your News Feed. There is no guarantee my information will be seen by my friends. Facebook controls information and uses an algorithm called Edge to determine what information they believe I want to see on my News Feed. There is a great business component with Pages (formally fan pages).

Google+
What makes you so different?

From a big picture perspective, g+ is all about connecting all of your computer uses, both online and offline, in one place. We are talking cloud on a major scale. We are talking about your documents, spreadsheets, applications, videos, everything being available in one location and everything being one click away from something you can share.

This brings us to the MAJOR DIFFERENCE of Google+

This is great—I can share all my information, from my blog to my expense report. But I don't want to share everything with the world. My friends don't need to know everything about my work, and my clients don't want to know about my personal life.

Google+ has created a revolutionary function called CIRCLES. Circles control both the stream of information out and in. People you connect with are organized into different circles.

How do Circles work and why are they important?

You can create any circle you want. Examples of circles include: Following, Friends, Best Friends, Employees, Clients, Vendors, Very Smart Marketing People, Fellow Legal Marketers, Funny Peeps and Family.

1. The people you connect with can be in multiple circles. Some people that are Very Smart Marketing People are also Friends.

2. You can choose to send information to one or more circles. This information will appear on their wall or can be sent as a message. The great thing is that if you share something with your client circle, only that circle—and no one else—sees that post on their feed. Let's say you just got back from a family vacation, and you want to share the photos with your family and friends but do not want to bother your vendors, clients and the general public with the images: this is easy with circles.

3. You can choose to see information from one or more circles in your feed. Instead of being told what content an algorithm thinks you would like to see, you can choose the content feed based on your own circles. This allows you to quickly and easily navigate from one set of feeds to the next. Since you can have people in multiple circles, you know that you are seeing what you want from whom you want.

Google+

Here are a few other features to Google+

- Multiple Video Chat: g+ will allow you to connect with up to 10 people on live video chat at the same time. The feature is smooth, and the audio is reliable. It's a really great way to connect with people for virtual meetings. The best part of this feature is the person talking gets the main screen with everyone else inside the videoconference reduced to a smaller video box located on the bottom of the screen. This is all done automatically through g+.

- Larger image and video display on the wall: When you post a video or image, they are about 3 times larger on the g+ wall in comparison with Facebook's old version (still being used by a few) and about 25% larger than Facebook's new Timeline.

- Easy navigation to all of Google's functions: While on g+, you can search the web, see your gmail messages and access your Google Documents.

- Simple share option: This is like Facebook in that Google uses both a +1 button (similar to Facebook's like) and a "share this post" option for spreading and endorsing content. You should be adding a +1 button and Facebook "Like" button to your blog.

- 1 click and you can add someone: If you see a name in a post, find someone in your friend's feed or stumble upon someone of interest, you can add them without navigating to their page. When you hover over their name, a box appears giving you the option to add them to a circle(s). This is a very convenient feature.

Setting up g+ is simple. Similar to other social media outlets, there is an area for information about you, pictures, website URLs and basic data. As always, only share what you are comfortable sharing. Make sure your "About Me" section has benefits to working with you and keywords for your industry. Like LinkedIn, there is a title area where you should also include keywords about your area of practice.

LinkedIn

In social media circles, LinkedIn is often completely overshadowed by its bigger social media cousins Facebook and Twitter. It is usually regarded as just a professional or resume-sharing site and nothing more. This is a big misstep for many, as LinkedIn is an enormous resource for prospects if used properly. For starters, LinkedIn itself is no slouch in terms of financial recognition; now publicly traded (LNKD), LinkedIn has a market cap of $8-$10 billion (or $70-$100 per user)—making it a very formidable, fast-growing contender in the social media sphere.

Additionally, LinkedIn has an added attraction to us that isn't related to its market share. Because of LinkedIn's status as a site for professionals and resume-swapping, the average LinkedIn user is far more likely to be a potential client because of the means / motive aspect we described earlier with Facebook. The following are demographics of LinkedIn users:

1. Over one fifth of users are middle management level or above.

2. Almost 60% have a college or post-graduate degree.

3. The Average Household Income is $88,573.

4. All of these numbers are higher than published statistics for Wall Street Journal, Forbes or BusinessWeek. This information is also found on

http://mashable.com/2012/03/09/social-media-demographics/. **For the most up-to-date information, visit** http://press.LinkedIn.com/.

Put simply, LinkedIn users are wealthier and have more need for services. Non-useful demographics, like teenagers, aren't crowding the LinkedIn user space to post pictures of their friends and pets. LinkedIn is composed of your potential clients interacting with each other, looking for professionals and just waiting to be introduced to your business.

The Four Major Parts to Your LinkedIn Profile:

This cuts to the core of LinkedIn and is part two of this series. Your LinkedIn profile is the mechanism that converts casual connections to future vendors, clients and partners.

A good rule of thumb is the 2 / 20 / 2 / 20 rule mentioned before.

You have 2 seconds to get someone's attention online; once you have their attention, you have 20 seconds to convince them to read more, and if they are still around, you have 2 minutes to earn their next 20 minutes.

The first stop on the 2 / 20 / 2 / 20 is your "Professional Headline." Often, you will see headlines that read like a job title: "Senior Vice President of the Product Group at XYZ Company."

Your Headline:

Your headline appears right under your name on LinkedIn and is your first opportunity to earn the next 20 seconds. This should be a thought-provoking, benefit-driven statement about what you do. For example, your headline could read: "Collaborative, Focused Divorce Attorney That Works Towards Mediation over Litigation."

When a prospect lands on your profile, they'll know exactly *how* what you do interacts with what their needs are. A headline like this also makes it easier for people to tell others what you do.

Your Summary:

This area is crucial to giving the person a reason to work with you. Most LinkedIn users will scroll down past the vital information to your summary. Your summary is your chance to brag. A friend of ours, J.D Gershbein (http://www.LinkedIn.com/in/jdgershbein) put it simply: "It is easier to talk positively about yourself in the third person than first person." This is a subtle thought with huge impact.

Your summary should read like a biography of achievements and benefits. "Insert your name has received X number of awards and industry recognition for their involvement in producing positive results for their clients...."

Generally, it is a good idea to keep your summary to three paragraphs or less.

Your Profile Video:

Since you followed our instructions in earlier chapters to the letter, you have a great video to post on your website. You can also use this video on your LinkedIn profile. It is easiest to embed the video from your YouTube account.

Your Recommendations:

Recommendations are a crucial part of the validation process on LinkedIn. You should have no less than five good recommendations. LinkedIn makes this simple by allowing you to send connections a recommendation request.

You should send a request to people that you believe will write a compelling recommendation. Remember that you can always delete a recommendation later if it doesn't quite fit your business model.

Those are the basics of a strong profile. Feel free to borrow any of the structural layout or style from my page: http://www.LinkedIn.com/in/jabezlebret

Connecting with People on LinkedIn:

LinkedIn is very picky about how you connect with people. They strongly discourage connecting with random people for random's sake. That being said, if there is a reason to connect with someone, by all means do, but be careful about connecting with every person you think would be a good connection. This policy is self-regulated by the LinkedIn community in the form of a spam button that people can and will use to alert LinkedIn that they do not appreciate your request to connect. The good news here concerns how to get around that issue and start connecting with everyone.

There are three main ways to connect with people on LinkedIn: we've done business together, groups or via email address.

The most important thing to know about connecting with people on LinkedIn—and the secret to almost completely avoiding a spam alert every time—is to connect with people with whom you share a group connection and to ALWAYS customize the invitation request.

The standard request is a horrible, tacky and lazy way to connect with people on LinkedIn. You do not need to write a novel; just one sentence will suffice, such as: "We both share a connection with the XYZ group, and I thought it would be nice to get connected here on LinkedIn. Looking forward to staying connected, Jabez LeBret"

Obviously, the above-mentioned strategy works only if you are connected in the same groups. Here is how to join and leverage LinkedIn groups.

LinkedIn Groups:

LinkedIn allows users to create groups to facilitate better connecting.

These include professional groups like Estate Planning Attorneys, association groups like Booth MBA Grads, interest groups like Dog Owners, etc. This is important to note, as you can build a plan for what kind of groups to join.

So, what kinds of groups should you join?

1. Target joining five to seven groups.

2. Each group should have 500 or more people.

3.   Groups should be active (at least 1 post a day).

Targeting the right group to join:

1.   Create a complete ideal client profile (include age, education, likes, dislikes, professions, hobbies, as much information as you can compile).

2.   Find 1 peer group that has the most members.

3.   Search for 4+ groups that match at least one component of your ideal client, e.g. MBA graduates that are in the financial industry.

How to Search for Groups:

You will find a search box in the upper right-hand corner of the page. This box has the option to search by group with the pull down tab. (FIGURE 20)

Just type in the keywords associated with your ideal client profile. This will pull up groups that have similar keywords in their group description. Take a look at the groups, and make sure they meet the requirements above before joining. Once you decide on a group, click "Join." Some groups require administrative approval to join. Don't worry: it is rare that you will be turned down from joining a group.

Figure 20. Linkedin Search Box

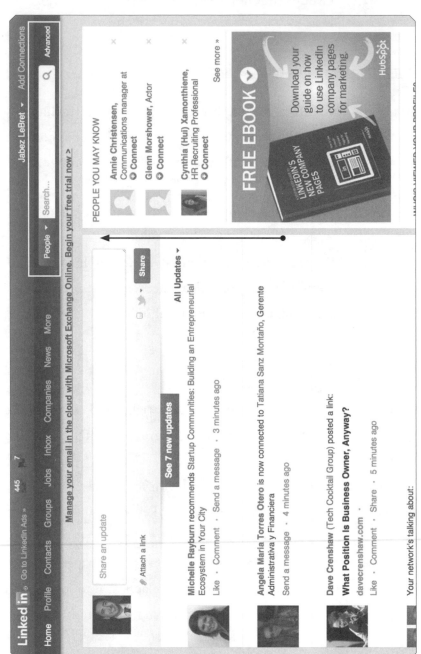

I've joined groups.
Now, how do I dominate LinkedIn
(in a polite way)?

The main function of groups is discussions. You will see a box where you can add a discussion to the group. These steps will help you get results quickly.

- **Discussions should be relevant to the group.** If you only post discussions that promote your business, you will quickly be ignored.

- **Comments drive discussion rankings.** More comments posted in a discussion lead to that discussion becoming the number one post. A great tip is to ask people you know in the group to add to your discussion.

- **Comment on your discussion when people comment.** The best thing you can do here is avoiding saying just, "Thanks;" say something compelling or that promotes follow-up commenting.

- **The discussion with the most recent and total comments gets emailed to the entire group.** This is huge. Some groups have tens of thousands of members. If you get a few comments and post responses to each, that is six total comments and usually enough to push you towards the top.

- **Post on other people's discussions.** Contributing will help people see that you are active, and that leads to more comments on your discussions.

> ◻ **Avoid flat-out pitching.** If you must, invite people to your blog, but do so sparingly. This is a place for information, not a sales pulpit.

A good thing to know is about 80% of your discussions or more are never going to receive comments. This happens to the best of us and shouldn't get you down. That is why you should post one new discussion per group per day (If you are in five groups, that would posting one discussion per day and that should take about 5-10 minutes per day).

Increased Visibility Through Discussions Inside Groups:

This is an amazing tool when used properly. A good discussion will have elements of intrigue and controversy. Remember, you do not have to take a stand to create controversy. Often, just asking the question is good enough, like: "When should we stop giving our kids trophies just for showing up?" (This was an actual discussion that grabbed over 80 comments.)

The important key to successful discussions is making the topic relevant to the audience in the group you are participating in without pitching or being self-serving.

Here Are a Few Tips About Posting Discussions:

DO post discussions regularly, about one discussion in each group a week. Each discussion can be a sentence or two long. That is only two sentences five times a week.

DO NOT post the same discussion on every group you are in because people, not so surprisingly, get annoyed at seeing the same discussion spamming every group.

Responding to Discussion Posts
Looking for Your Services:

When you come across a discussion that says anything to the effect of "Looking for information on (insert your knowledge area here)," you need to be prepared to market yourself.

There will be a ton of people pursuing this client, and you won't stand a chance if you are unprepared or lazy.

Here Are a Few Tips for Answering These Posts:

DO research the person. Email them directly, either through LinkedIn or through their website.

DO NOT just reply with a comment on the discussion with one or two lines telling the person you are "perfect" or "interested—please tell me more." In fact, don't reply with a comment at all. You should message them directly off the discussion board.

Other Social Networks:

There are literally hundreds of social networks, and, of course, we are not going to spend time on every one of them. But there are a couple you should keep your eye on, and one that you may be interested in joining for fun. (Yes, you are allowed to still have fun with this online stuff.)

Here are the latest and greatest to enter the fray of social media:

Pinterest – This social network focuses on images and provides users the ability to "pin," or post an image, to their own "pin board," or wall. Then, you can look through images on other people's boards or search for images via keywords. It's the fastest growing social network *ever*! This social media network is also able to boast the largest number of click-throughs (people visiting websites via the images they see). This social network is comprised mostly of bloggers and women. If either of those are your target market, you should strongly consider getting involved with this network.

Quora: This social network attempts to bring people with questions together with people that have answers. Users determine what answers are the best answers by providing a thumbs up or thumbs down. This site turns out to be a great resource for both finding prospects and discovering very intelligent answers to some thought-provoking questions. It's not only a great place to hang out every once in a while and give a few answers but also a perfect place to do some research about hobbies or professional topics. It's not really a major player, but this site has attracted some of the brightest minds— making it worth a mention..

With social media shifting and changing so rapidly, the information in this chapter is certain to update within the next year. This is the difficult part of social media. We've created an area where you can go to get the most up-to-date information about social media and the changes to the various networks.

Please visit our blog for the latest news on social media changes:

---

http://www.GetNoticedGetFound.com/blog

We could go on for a whole book just on social media, but that's not the purpose of this book. What we have shown you in this chapter is the minimum work you should be doing to harness the strength of social media for SEO. There is, of course, people that will preach about getting business through social media, and we agree there is value there. What this book is striving to do is help you establish a web presence that drives traffic to your website. With that, our foray into social media has ended; next up on our list is directory listings!

- Despite the somewhat laughable reputation that social media has, it is still an extremely useful and important part of your online presence.

- Because people don't share information that they don't like, Google realizes that information found on social media sites is most likely relevant and important—giving it a lot of ranking credit.

- Focus on Facebook, Twitter, Google+ and LinkedIn, though you may want to have a presence on other sites as well, like Pinterest or Quora.

- On Facebook, create a business page (NOT the same as or connected to your personal page) to link to your website, increase your brand awareness and get new clients. Use Facebook to link to your blog posts, not write about what your breakfast was that morning.

- Google indexes *every single tweet* on Twitter. Tweet about the same kind of legal and local content you'd write about in a blog—just shortened to 140 characters or less. Build your following on Twitter to get people to "re-tweet" or share your tweets.

- Google+: Share relevant information with the "Circles" you choose, link to your website and blog posts and include your keywords and benefits to working with you in the "About Me" section.

- LinkedIn may be much more likely to have potential clients because it is a website for professionals and those in need of services. Create a personal Linkedin profile and a company page (both of which should have attention-grabbing, benefit-driven headlines as well as video and recommendations). In addition, join and interact with groups!

- Check with your state bar association to ensure that your social media strategy complies with their regulations.

CHAPTER 8

Directory Listings:

Setting Up Your Listings, Listings to Use and Others to Avoid

I f you've been an Internet user since the pre-search days, you'll recognize directory listings. Directory listings are, in short, the online version of the yellow pages: your business name, address and phone number, on sites like Super Pages, YellowPages.com, Yahoo Local, Bing Places, Google+ Local, etc. These directory listings are commonly called "citations" by those in the Internet marketing and search marketing industry.

There are hundreds of them across the Internet; there are, however, 12-15 major ones where you want to be listed. In addition to the main directories like MerchantCircle.com, SuperPages.com, Yelp.com and Yahoo Local, attorneys should be sure to get listed on AVVO.com. Certain directories, like InfoUSA, are more influential than others because other directories pull information from them. In time, as other directories use the information listed there, your information will proliferate all over the Internet. Because your information will often spread from one directory to another, it is crucial to make sure that this information is correct and optimized in the most important and influential ones.

The majority of these services allow for a free listing. You should not need anything more than that. Resist the urge to listen to emails and phone calls trying to upsell you into a paid option. A paid listing or preferred listing may be right for you, depending on your market, but register with all the free ones first. After you have a baseline for your online success, test the gain in calls or emails you receive by opting for a paid enhancement to a directory listing. This way, you can measure the real cost/benefit of the investment.

These directories/citations have risen to prominence lately because of Google's local search policies—since Google has moved its local search returns to its main page using Google+ Local. The algorithm that determines which Google+ Local business listings belong on the first page of Google's search results takes a great deal of its ranking consideration from directory listings around the web. If you're in 5, 10, 15 or even 35+ directory listings (with reviews in your local area), that's going to look very good to Google's ranking system. We'll get to reviews in the next chapter, but for now, it is sufficient to say that directory listings with reviews are very helpful. If your competition is getting more reviews than you, you often won't make the first page, and they will!

You're going to want to be on a great many directories; there are some services out there that will do this automatically for you, but quite often, the best way to do this is manually. Some services are pretty spotty, and they'll slip in shady techniques or insist that you stay out of the process. It's not that hard or time-consuming, and you'll want to be in control of the process, so we recommend doing it manually. Simply start with the top 10-15 Directory Listings, enter in your data, upload photos, and fill out the details as much as you can. Make sure to use keywords and a geo-location in your description. For example, if you're an elder law attorney and your keywords are "VA benefits," you could put in your description "VA benefits lawyer in Dallas, Texas."

How to List Yourself
Doing this wrong can ruin your online presence and overall strategy

It's a pretty easy process to list yourself, all things considered: you just have to go to these directories and their websites and list your business. Some are paid, but many are free and will later try to up-charge you with different services once you've listed yourself on the directories. You may be conflicted about these upcharges and paid directory listings, but they're really not necessary. Our experience is that, done correctly, you never need to pay for directory listings or any of the extra services the free ones offer you; judicious and skillful use of keywords and geo-location will be more than enough to bump you up to the top. We've had many, many clients achieve top ranking in Google+ Local who never paid for directory listings, and it's most likely the case that you'll never have to pay for a directory listing or upcharge either. That is not to say that these additional paid services won't provide more traffic and clients to your business, but you don't need to start there.

Be warned: You should be prepared for multiple phone calls from directories looking to sell you upcharges and service add-ons. Changes to Google and other advertising venues online have left many of these directories scrambling to rethink their business models. Paying for a directory listing is no longer as necessary as it used to be. You'll have many directories telling you to upcharge this and upcharge that and pay for advertising, but don't do it: stay steadfast, keep on trucking, and you'll see that it wasn't necessary at all to pay for any services that the directory listings tried to offer you!

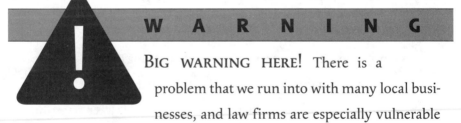

WARNING

BIG WARNING HERE! There is a problem that we run into with many local businesses, and law firms are especially vulnerable to it. What happens quite frequently is that, in a law office, you have 3-4 attorneys that are really in one office partnership. Sometimes, each attorney will create their own listings, so you end up with multiple listings for each attorney and one for the office as a whole. When Google queries the directory listings, it gets confused by the multiple entries for one address; it thinks it's an attempt to game the system and may ignore them all.

You want to be very, very careful that you have only one listing. Search for your address, business name and other people in the office, anything you can think of to find and identify multiple listings. If you do have multiple listings, delete them all except one. Get down to one, and start from scratch: it's much better that way.

It used to be a big trick to list duplicate listings to boost search rankings, but now Google cracks down on this practice. Remember: Duplicate listings are harmful to your ranking! Too many duplicates, and Google completely ignores them all. Be very wary of this, and search hard to find and delete duplicate listings!

This goes for all directory and citation websites. This is also the reason you need to be careful about a service that says they will automatically add you to 20 directories. Some of these services work—we have agency status with one company—but many times, they will simply add duplicate listings, which can ruin your whole presence.

Another important thing to remember when you're doing directory listings is to make sure to use keywords and geo-location only in the short and long descriptions given in the listing. Do not use keywords in your business name. Google does not like to see business names stuffed with keywords and geo-location, so this will definitely hurt you in the long run.

This can be turned to your advantage, depending on how dedicated you are to the strategy of adding keywords; some of our sharper clients have actually changed their business name to include keywords and geo-location, like "Elder Law of Georgia Firm." (This may recall the Yellow Pages game of putting A's in business names to get to the top of the listings, like "A Best Dentist of Dallas, Texas".)

If your company name officially contains your keywords and location, Google is okay with that; what they're watching out for is obvious keyword stuffing like "Jones Smith and Barney Attorneys at Law - estate planning - elder law - va benefits - dallas tx." This is bad practice: those keywords should go in your description, not in your business name.

Think about what 411 directory service would say your business name is, and use that.

! WARNING

THE INFORMATION ON every directory and citation site must identically match the information on your website, other directory listings and 411. Some companies will try to sell you tracking numbers that forward to your office phone. This is a great idea for measuring exactly how many people are calling you from your website or Google+ Local page. Trust us, as a firm that always has to show our clients their return on investment, we wish that tracking numbers could be used. The issue is that the tracking number on your website doesn't match the phone number for your office in the 411 directory. When Google and other search engines try to validate your phone number, they often reach out to 411 or InfoUSA. When Google sees two different numbers, they get confused. When the search engines get confused, you drop in the ranking. This is why tracking numbers are so dangerous. Google will crawl the web, trying to validate your business, and it will find your tracking number in one place and your real number in the directory listings. When this happens, Google will get confused, assume you are trying to pull something questionable and drop you in the ranking. We have witnessed this firsthand with clients, and this is well known in the SEO community. Companies like YP.com and FindLaw will tell you otherwise; flat out, they are wrong. Every listing should have the exact same firm name, address, phone number and URL. The only thing that can vary from one listing to the next is your firm description. Having listings that do not match your website and information is a sure way to guarantee that your competition will pass you in the ranking, or worse, that you will end up on page 39, trying to claw your way back to page 1.

If the directory listing has suggested keywords, consider using them. They probably look very similar to the Yellow Pages categories you are used to seeing. Some listing services give you a chance to type in your own keywords, in which case you should do so. Don't go crazy with the keywords, however, because Google only values about 3-4 keywords; anything after that they consider gaming the system, and you will be ignored.

There are a ton of directory sites (into the hundreds). Some are better than others, and to be fair, they change from time to time. For a current listing of the top directories that we use for our clients, see the link below.

To get the directory listings, go to...

w w w . G e t N o t i c e d G e t F o u n d . c o m / d i r e c t o r i e s

Google+ Local:

Google+ Local (formerly Google Places), though technically a listing, deserves special mention here. The Google+ Local listing should be the absolute last thing you should create; get the rest of the directory listings in first, wait a week or so or until you have a few reviews, then create your Google+ Local page.

The reason behind this is that, when you create a Google+ Local page, Google goes forth and looks for information about you: directory listings, blogs, reviews and so forth. If you've done all the things we've talked about, you should rocket way up to the top of the list once you create your Google+ Local page; if you want to be on the first page, waiting those few days to make a Google+ Local listing makes a huge, huge difference in your ranking.

With the blending of Google+ and Google Places, the overall layout of this listing has changed significantly. If you already have a Google+ Local page, make sure to check this directory to ensure that your images have been re-sized properly to accommodate the recent changes.

Here are the components of your Google+ Local page that you should add:

1. Images of your firm. These should all be from your website or Panoramio. Add the maximum number of images the system will let you.

2. Description of your practice. Add a complete description of your firm, including benefits, statements about how you help clients, keywords, geo-location and your firm name.

3. Video from YouTube. Since you can add videos, you should add both your home page video and at least one video from your 10 frequently asked questions.

4. Keywords / Category: Add your categories, e.g. Attorney, Estate Planning, Divorce, Law Firm

5.   Get people to review your firm on Google+ Local. This is so important that we have a whole chapter dedicated to getting reviews (coming up next).

We are not going to go into depth on this topic, but another powerful yet rarely discussed advertising medium is Pay Per Click (PPC) advertising—the best example of which is Google AdWords. AdWords is pound-for-pound the single quickest way to get your firm listed on Page #1 of Google. You can do it in 10 minutes or less. It will cost you a few dollars a day (when you know what you are doing). Or it could cost you thousands (if you don't). The key is to have your ads show ONLY in your geographical area. Our recommendation is to find someone who is skilled at AdWords and pay them to do your ads. It will pay off for you in the end.

- Directory listings (also called "citations") are the online version of the yellow pages and include your firm name, phone number, and address.

- There are hundreds of directory listings, but you don't need to be listed on *all* of them. Major listings where you should be listed include Google+ Local, Yahoo Local, Yelp, YellowPages.com, and AVVO.com.

- The information that you put in each citation will proliferate all over the web, so make sure that everything that you include—down to the last punctuation mark—is consistent with your website information, correct and optimized!

- Manually entering citations are the best way to ensure that your information is correct.

- Be very careful that you do not have duplicate or incorrect listings—Google's algorithm will be confused by the misinformation and WILL penalize you by dropping your website's ranking for this.

- Use keywords in each citation—but do so carefully. Don't keyword-stuff, particularly in your business name.

- Don't use tracking numbers—these numbers won't match your firm's phone number and will confuse Google, leading to a drop in rankings!

- Google+ Local is the most important listing you can have, as it can make a huge difference in your ranking! Be sure to add images, keywords, video, a description of your firm and reviews!

- You'd don't need to pay for citations. Do all of the free ones first, and if paid listings are right for your firm, then continue to those.

Notes

CHAPTER 9

Getting Reviews:

How They Single-Handedly Drive Your Search Ranking

T his part of the system really confuses some people, especially since reviews are created by clients and customers. How can reviews make or break a search engine ranking? Certainly, they might be helpful for clients talking to clients, but surely they can't influence Google's monstrous ranking machine in your favor... can they?

As it turns out, they can and they do influence the ranking system. Very much so, in fact: Google uses reviews in order to judge the validity of the business in question. Put simply, if the location has been reviewed, someone's been there. In addition, the review comments give an indication of the quality of the location and whether or not it deserves to be ranked higher or lower. Many of these reviews allow reviewers to give star ratings or a 30 out of 30, which are even more influential: Google scrapes these numbers automatically to do a sort of website litmus test, a judgment of whether or not the establishment is viewed positively or negatively overall.

In fact, Google has recently adjusted the Google+ Local page user interface to prominently display the "Write a review" button to specifically encourage reviews within Google's own systems.

(FIGURE 21)

Review sites are, in general, the directory listings we talked about earlier. Google uses the info to determine whether or not you're the best solution to the problem the user is trying to solve. This is important because the whole idea of the ranking system and your marketing strategy is to make Google see that you are, in fact, the best solution to the problem.

Another key point to this strategy is that many of your competitors are simply not getting reviews at all. This is especially true in the Internet marketing strategies of law firms; we've done extensive research specifically with attorneys, and hardly any of them receive reviews, as evidenced by this Google+ Local page:

(FIGURE 22)

This law firm, though it has a Google+ Local page, has no reviews attached to it at all. You can see that you don't need to get a billion reviews on your directory listings and Google+ Local page to win out over your competitors; you just need to have a little consistency, making sure that you get a couple reviews a month on just 2 or 3 different directories (one of which must be Google+ Local).

Figure 21. Google+ Local With Arrow Pointing To Write A Review

Figure 22 Google Review Returns Showing Low Number Of Reviews

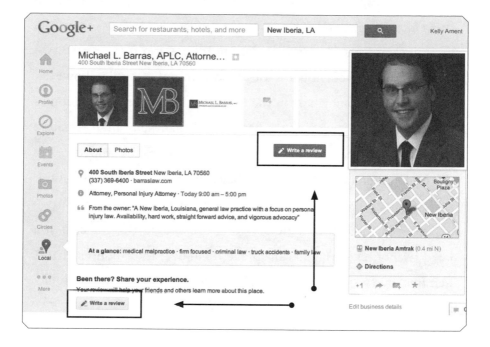

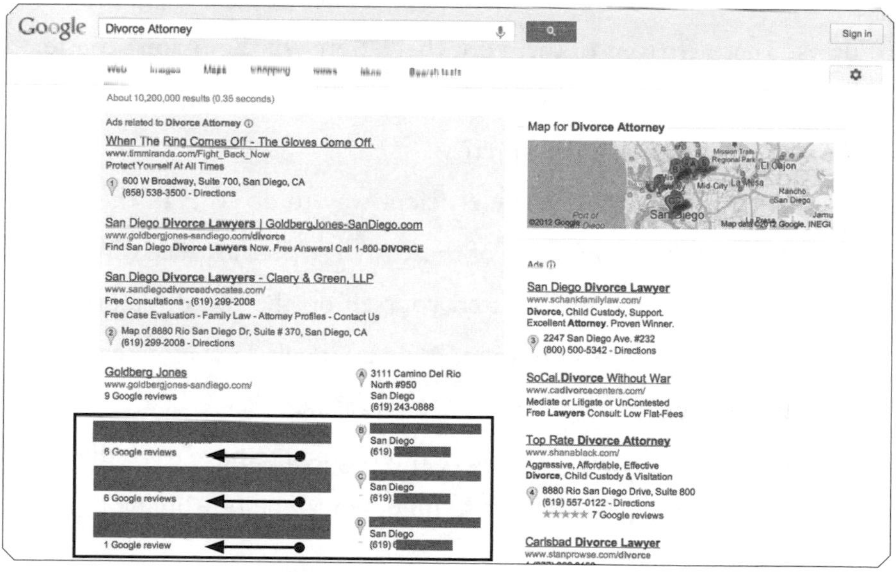

To start, you're going to need to determine how many reviews you need to rank. Do some review research on your keywords; type them into Google, and see how many reviews the top ranked results have. If they have five reviews, you need ten, and if they have two hundred, well... you've got a lot of work to do! Typically, however, attorneys have somewhere in the ten to twenty range when it comes to number of reviews (and we have found that many markets don't have any). For the most part, in order to beat your competitors at the rankings game, you'll need to have about double the amount of reviews they have.

Keep in mind that these are total reviews: for example, if you need twenty reviews, you can spread them over four months. That's just five reviews per month, which is certainly doable, and we'll talk about how to get those reviews in a second.

Review Sites

First things first: which sites should you focus on when getting reviews? There are tons of them out there. Some of them don't matter, and some of them do. How do you figure out which ones are worth your time and which ones aren't?

Thankfully, there's a fairly efficient way to do it. Half the work is already done for you: many of these review sites are also directory listings, and you've already listed yourself on the top directory listings. What you have to do, then, is do a Google keyword search in your location and go through the search results.

Don't go digging too far: you're rarely going to have to go digging down through the pages. If you scroll down to the bottom, you'll see numbers as far as the mouse can click. For your part, you're just interested in the top 5 directories that are already listed. Cross-reference which ones appear first in the Google keyword search with a list of your directory listings. For example, if you are a Divorce Attorney in Pittsburgh, PA, then you should Google "Divorce Attorney Pittsburgh PA – your firm name." Then, look at the results, and find the first 3-5 listings that refer to an online directory site like Yelp, Citysearch or Superpages. When you search, the top 3-5 listings that you find are the ones you're going to want to focus on.

It's also okay if you don't find 5; you may only find 2 or 3 at the beginning. This is normal: sometimes it can take search engines quite some time to properly index all the information out there. To give you some perspective, there are about ten thousand new websites created every day. This is a gigantic amount of information for search engines to index, so there is often a lag time as the search engines crawl the pages and index them. Your mission here is to find the ones that are ranked, and, of those, find the top ranked ones; these are the ones where you're going to focus your review techniques.

IF THERE ARE a large number of reviews for your keyword niche, consider focusing on one or two directory sites for your clients to give your firm a review. Ordinarily, attorneys don't have to deal with this since the attorney market isn't normally saturated with reviews. If you have a competitor

that's saturated with reviews, however, Google their keywords to see which review sites are consistently being pulled up the most; focus all your review efforts on those. As an example, if your keyword is "VA benefits San Francisco California" and the majority of reviews are being pulled from Citysearch and Findlaw, then Citysearch and Findlaw are the best places to start.

Getting Reviews

Now that we've narrowed down our target directories, let's get reviews on them. We'll start with your current clients: it'll be easier to get reviews from them because they're right in the middle of working with you.

It's important to note that we understand that attorneys are, depending on the state, not allowed to ask for testimonials. However, it is essential that you understand that you are not asking for a testimonial. We are very clear on this point: you are simply asking for someone to go to a website and put in a review. It's on a public forum where they could leave the review with or without your assistance. You'll want to have a card produced (see our sample below) that you hand to your clients as they walk out the door; this card will tell them where to go and how to write a review. This is absolutely crucial. (FIGURE 23)

Figure 23. Sampler Review Cards

THANK YOU FOR BEING A TRUSTED CLIENT OF OURS.
Please take a few moments to log into one of these sites and write a quick a review; this will be of great service to us.

www.Yelp.com/YourFirm

www.google.places.com/YourFirm

www.merchantcircle.com/YourFirm

local.yahoo.com/YourFirm

If you have any questions

please contact us directly at:

555.555.5555

Note - Here is a definition of the ranking system:

★ ★ ★ ★ ★ You enjoyed working with us

★ ★ ★ ★ Our services met your expectations

★ ★ ★ We could have done better

★ ★ There were problems with our service

★ We completely let you down

SAMPLE REVIEWS FOR YOUR REFERENCE:

• "The service was polite and they really made a difficult circumstance comfortable. I am so glad we went to..."

• "I have been working with YOUR FIRM for years and I am glad to have you in my corner and on my side, thanks for always getting done what you promise"

• "At first I was unsure if I needed any firm. After a few visits I am so glad I chose YOUR FIRM. Not only did I need a firm, YOUR FIRM made the whole process painless."

W A R N I N G

YOU CANNOT, UNDER any circumstances, go to a website and create reviews. Falsifying reviews is illegal. Your clients also cannot give you the reviews in a letter and have you write the reviews for them from your computer; Google will know from the IP address (the address of your computer and your office Wi-Fi) that these reviews are all coming from the same location. They will ignore these reviews, at best, or hurt your ranking or get rid of your listing altogether, at worst. This is true even if the reviews are real reviews that clients mailed you: a common scammer trick is to have teams of people write multiple (false) reviews, and because of this, Google searches that spam out and penalizes it harshly. **Under no circumstances should your clients write reviews from your location: they have to go to their computer at their house, business or coffee shop and write the review there. This is vital.**

This also extends to other computers in your office. A common setup we see fairly often is firms having a "review" computer set up in the office where clients can go and enter in a review. This falls into the same trap as the scenario above, and we always warn clients against this when we see it: Even though it's not you typing, unfortunately, it's coming from the same place. As Google tracks these reviews, it can't distinguish these from scammers who employ that same trick. Thus, having this "review station" isn't going to help your rank at all. The reviewers absolutely, positively have to do it on their computer in their home or business; there's no way around this, and it's very important for you to remember this!

⚠ W A R N I N G

BE VERY, VERY, very careful about who you hire to do your review process! There are many services out there that will solicit you and claim to be able to get you lots of reviews. Very often, these services are the spamming type of businesses that creates all the reviews themselves and posts them from one IP address; not only is this not going to help you, this sort of review fabrication is against the law. You have to be very careful about who you consult and how. If you talk to a company that says they'll get you twenty reviews in a week, you should be very cautious. We've even seen fake reviews from firms we've worked with that have used such services. Google can really tell these reviews are faked, and that is in violation of every online company's terms of services. The worse part is that when you hire a company to provide reviews, if they cheat the system, you are held liable by both the online community and your bar association.

Do not use a service! If you absolutely must, make sure you build your process with a proven agency or partner. We provide our clients with a complete review process and require them to ask for the reviews from their real clients for the reasons outlined above. You must guard your online presence—in the end, it is you and your firm that is held responsible for what is published in your name.

As an example of this, we have a process in which we do the calling and mailers for our clients, depending on their individual needs. We keep close communication with the client and have an active role in the process due to the nature, sensitivity and importance of reviews. This is how your service, if you use one, should treat you. Make sure the service keeps in regular contact with your firm and ultimately gives you control over the review process. This is a crucial part of hiring a service—don't forget it when you're looking around for these agencies or services.

The best way to get these reviews, as mentioned above, is to hand out your card. Don't stop there, however: another great way to do this is mail or email clients asking for reviews (see our sample below). Make it a team effort by inserting into the email where you're ranking in comparison with your competitors and explaining that you want to get to the top with your reviews.

(Figure 24)

Note that this isn't all about Google+ Local—we want to send people to a few different directories. You do, of course, want reviews going to Google+ Local, but you also need to diversify: have cards requesting reviews on other sites as well, such as Yelp, CitySearch and the others that you've identified in your target directory listings. Try not to put them all on one card. It looks cramped, awkward and unprofessional. A card per review site looks much more professional and will work better in getting clients to go to the review sites for you.

The same goes for your emails. Your clients may already have an account on one of these directory sites where they can leave you a review, and it could be easy for them to leave a review saying what a wonderful job you did. This helps your ranking even more as identified reviews count more than anonymous ones.

Again, it's important to note that these are absolutely, positively not testimonials: these are reviews that consumers can do on their own. In fact, you're only trying to encourage a behavior that's already happening: don't be surprised if, when you start this process, you find that you already have a couple of reviews scattered around the Internet. You're simply saying to your clients: "Hey, there are these review sites out there, and having reviews help us. You might do it

Figure 24. Review Sample Email

SUBJECT:
On a warm summer day I can't think of anything better to do...

BODY:
This email may not be on top of your list of things to do on a sunny day, but connecting with our best clients is on our list. We are writing you today to say hello and wish you the best. As part of our efforts to continue to provide the best service to our clients, we would like to ask you for a quick favor.

Please take a moment to go to one of the websites below and leave us a review. This will help us improve and grow as a firm. We want to say thank you in advance for your loyalty as a client.

To make things simple, below are a few samples, and here is a quick guide to the review process:

Here is a definition of the ranking system:
* We completely let you down
* * There were problems with our service
* * * We could have done better
* * * * Our services met your expectations
* * * * * You enjoyed working with us

Visit one of these two sites:
http://www.ReviewSiteNumber1.com/YourFirm
http://www.ReviewSiteNumber2.com/YourFirm

Again, thank you.

Best Wishes,
FIRM NAME
FirmWebsite.com

Sample Review For Your Reference: *(feel free to copy and paste if you would like)*

"The service was polite and they really made a difficult circumstance comfortable. I am so glad we went to..."

"I have been working with YOUR FIRM for years and I am glad to have you in my corner and on my side, thanks for always getting done what you promise"

"At first I was unsure if I needed any firm. After a few visits I am so glad I chose YOUR FIRM. Not only did I need a firm YOUR FIRM made the whole process painless."

already, and if you liked our service, your review will really help our Internet ranking and get more people into our door!"

You'll find that, more often than not, people are more than willing to help you out in this regard: they'll go to these sites and fill out reviews. It's one of the driving forces behind Google+ Local rankings, and by having this steady system of reviews, you're ensuring your steady climb to the top.

Getting reviews is key. To see some "behind the scenes" strategies on how we currently get reviews on behalf of our clients, go to the link below. Warning: this stuff works, so be prepared for an influx of clients. Can you take it? Kidding…

To get the review process, go to…

(as always no email required)

www.GetNoticedGetFound.com/reviewwhitepaper

- Reviews can and do influence Google's (and other search engine's) ranking system! Reviews provide validity that your business is real and give search engines an indication of your business' worthiness to be ranked highly.

- As an attorney, you will need about twice as many reviews as the competitors in your keyword niche. Most attorneys, unless they are in a very competitive area, need only around 10-20 reviews.

- Since most review sites are also directory sites, you only need to search the top directory sites for your keywords and get reviews there. You should get reviews on several different sites—this MUST include your Google+ Local page.

- Faking reviews is illegal and will not fool Google: you will be ignored or even penalized in the rankings for having fake reviews. You also should not have a "review computer" in your office for clients to leave reviews: since the reviews will come from one IP address, Google will assume that they are scams, ignore them and penalize you. Clients MUST leave reviews from their own computer in their home, office or elsewhere—not in your office.

- Beware of companies that offer to get your firm reviews fast! Many "services" that promise a large amount of reviews in little time are scammers that write fake reviews, and you will be held responsible for what they write in your name.

- Reviews are NOT testimonials; you are simply encouraging a behavior that people already do. To ask your clients for reviews, hand out cards (one for each review site) with the link to your listing.

Notes

CHAPTER 10

Follow-up Strategies and Automation

Follow-up strategies are a vital segment of any Internet marketing strategy, and it's equally vital that you automate them as much as possible. Many firms will try to do this manually, but the overhead required to manually implement isn't feasible for most firms. Don't spend time fielding emails and responding one by one; we've had clients in the past who literally sent out e-mail newsletters every week. If somebody new came in, they would be manually added to this email list. That sort of system may work in the beginning, but it's easy to see that it doesn't scale up well at all. You need an automated method of follow-up that both preserves quality and also scales up well, freeing up resources and keeping your internet marketing strategy running smoothly and efficiently.

Follow-up Framework

First, we have to talk about the framework for follow-up: when we're talking about follow-up, we're talking about new prospects that resulted from traffic to your website. We're not talking about people that come in through the door, necessarily; we're talking about follow-up that happens when the person finds you online. You need a follow-up strategy whether or not the contact is initiated by phone, email or online via the website.

When a new prospect gets to your website and chooses to give their name, phone number and email address, they go into your funnel. These prospects have gone through the trouble of giving you this information, so they're a "warm lead:" they are obviously interested, and you have to get to them fast before they cool off. Your funnel is the resource where you capture your leads and market to them specifically from there. The whole function of the funnel is to provide you with a resource that enables this sort of rapid response to whatever communication the client happened to initiate.

The best way to do this is to set up a basic auto-responder system. This system will provide two things to you: it will alert you that someone has given you information, and it will send them a message immediately. There are a couple of ways to do this, and we'll talk later on about different techniques, including texting and direct voicemail. The most traditional and common auto-response, however, is an email, and that's something they should be getting immediately. A typical auto-response email could look something like this:

(FIGURE 25)

FIGURE 25. SAMPLE EMAIL IMAGE

From: **Victoria Collier** <info@estateplanningattorneyatlantaga.com>
Date: Mon, Apr 25, 2011 at 5:08 PM
Subject: The 7 Things You Must Know Before Hiring an Elder Law Attorney
To: jabez.lebret@gmail.com

Hi Jabez,

Thank you for taking the initiative to sign up for my free report on the 7 Things You Must Know Before Hiring An Elder Law Attorney.

As you know, here at our firm we have a passion for helping people just like you to protect their assets, help their parents, get the benefits they are due, and manage all aspects of their future.

This is such an important decision that we wanted to ensure you were making an educated one. So please, shut the door and turn off the phone and take a moment to really understand this report and how it impacts your decision.

And that brings me to the point of today's e-mail which is to show you where to get your free report.

On the page below, you will find...

The 7 Things You Must Know Before Hiring Any Attorney.

http://estateplanningattorneyatlantaga.com/SpecialReport/

All The Best,

Collier & St. Clair, LLP
(404) 381-8004
http://estateplanningattorneyatlantaga.com

That's an example of something a prospect should be getting immediately after they submit their information on your web page. There are many services out there that provide these types of auto-responding systems: Constant Contact, AWeber, InfusionSoft, Instant Customer, etc. Whichever service you go with, you have to make absolutely sure that they have a system in place capable of capturing names, storing names in an organized way and making it as easy and automated as possible to send out those auto-responders.

You also need to have a strategy in place for phone numbers. If someone gives you their phone number, you should not only email that person right away but also email someone in your office a note that says: "Hey, this person called that is interested in this. Here's their number." The reason for this is the Internet is 24 hours: it doesn't close, it's always open, and your website is happily receiving visitors all around the clock. Your office hours, however, are only during the day, and if your office hours are from nine to four, for example, you won't be answering phones at ten in the evening.

If someone visits your website at night and submits their information, they get an immediate email; when your person gets in the next morning at nine, they can see the email and know someone tried to get in touch. They can then pick up the phone and say, "Hey, this is Bob Jones from Jones, Smith, and Johnson. I saw you downloaded our special report, and I hope it helped you out. I'm just calling to ask if there's anything we can help you with." This is a very personal follow-up to a warm lead, with an emphasis on the personal. We can't stress that enough; you're a local business providing a service to the community, and you need to reach out and make those personal connections. The bigger the step, the better, and an automated email is the minimum bar to entry. If they've gone through the trouble of giving you their email, you need to say thanks, email back and throw in a special report—maybe email them again a few days later with another message. You should have a few templates for these emails that you can send out to your warm leads.

It's very important to implement this email / phone call system and use it regularly. This isn't e-commerce, and you are not going to close any deals online. There's no shopping cart, no impulse buy button that's going to magically give you clients without any legwork, especially in the legal industry. You are still a local business engaged in local Internet marketing, so you can't just send out an email and expect things to happen. You need to get that phone call or office visit to seal the deal!

Another good best practice is to email out one of your blog posts per month. Just take one of your blog posts each month, any one of them, and fire it out to everyone on your email lists. It's very easy to send out what's called a "broadcast message" to everyone on your email list still marked as open to receiving communication from you. You'll want to do this to establish a long-term strategy; your clients may be thinking they need legal services, but they may not need them quite yet. That doesn't mean, however, that they won't need them down the line, and these periodic emails will remind them of your business. This is called "top of mind awareness" in marketing; you want to be on the top of the mind to a client down the road. They may one day think, "Oh! My dad needs info about his VA benefits. I've been getting these emails from a firm down the road who deals with this sort of thing. Maybe I'll give them a call and see if they can answer my questions!"

- Your "funnel" is the place where leads enter and where you market to them. People enter your Internet marketing funnel by giving you their information, such as their email address or phone number, via your website.

- To have your Internet marketing work as smoothly and efficiently as possibly, you need to automate some of your follow-up systems so that they scale well and preserve quality; manually responding to every email just isn't feasible.

- Set up an auto-responder system, which will both alert you that someone has contacted you and immediately respond to that lead. If a person emails you, they should get an email in return. If they give you their phone number, someone from your office should know to call them.

- Services that provide auto-responders include Constant Contact, AWeber, InfusionSoft, Instant Customer

- You can also send out periodic emails about your blog posts to everyone on your email lists; this will keep you at the top of their mind.

- It's important to have follow-up systems in place to provide personal service and make sure that your firm is at the top of potential clients' minds. Even if they don't need your services now, they may need them in the future—and you want them to think of you.

Understanding the ROI:

How to Track Expenses and Returns for the Dollars that You Spend

I n the typical budget that we've seen from clients we've worked with, the vast majority of advertising dollars get spent in the yellow pages, radio and possibly a few TV ads. A lot of attorneys are not spending enough money online and if they are, it's an extension of the yellow pages that is usually not well-tracked and often very ineffective.

Advertising online, however, has a huge advantage over traditional advertising methods normally used by most firms: it's extraordinarily easy to track what's going on throughout the entire online process. You can track quite well what's happening in each stage of the game: who emailed you, what's in the funnel for leads, what's going on with your analytics and so forth. This is very difficult to do with regular advertising; quite often, the only method of communication that traditional advertising media gives a firm is the client phone number. Unless you're asking each person where they heard about you or creating a unique phone number for each ad (which is, by the way, a very good best practice: more on that later), you're not getting very good information at all about how your advertising budget is helping you!

In contrast with these traditional advertising methods, there are amazingly vast amounts of data you can glean from the Internet and the tools available to you. You can track how many people visit and what keywords they typed in that led them to click your website. If they visit your Google+ Local page, you can have instant knowledge there, including who visited, when and how. Some directory listings have tracking data in place as well. The big Kahuna in the realm of tracking, however, is Google Analytics.

Google Analytics is an absolute must-have for your website. If it's not already on your website, ask your webmaster to integrate Google Analytics with your site. If they can't, it's time to find another webmaster. That's how important Google Analytics is to your Return On Investment, or ROI. It tells you who's visiting, who's clicking, what data they're entering, how well your website is converting leads, how long your clients stay on your site and more. (FIGURE 26)

FIGURE 26. GOOGLE ANALYTICS IMAGE

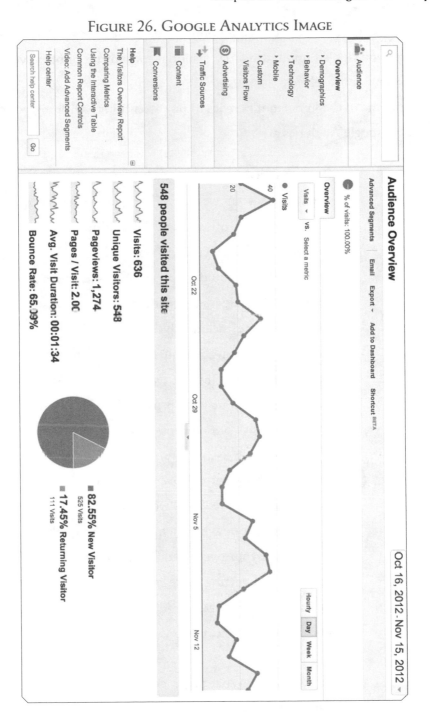

Because of the extensive amount of data the Google Analytics gives you, it's an unquestionably essential tool for monitoring your ROI and your website.

Some of the important metrics to pay attention to with regard to your Google Analytics are:

1.   **Time on site:** How long each user is staying, on average, on your website. This number needs to be above 1 or 2 minutes, at the minimum. If this number is too low, you will not achieve rankings, or worse, you could have a serious conversion problem. Possible issues that are causing low time on the website include the following: too many busy graphics, too difficult to navigate, topics on the site don't match what was searched, too little information about the prospect's needs, unattractive website or takes too long to load website.

2.   **Number of visitors:** How many people visited your website over the last week, month and quarter. Do not get bogged down with daily numbers: think about your overall traffic in weekly chunks. Whether you getting more or less visitors is a key indicator of your ranking. Ranking higher will lead to more traffic, period.

3.   **Pages visited:** What pages people navigate to and what pages they leave your website from. You can

see both the page they visited and get an "Exit" percentage. If you find that people tend to navigate to a random page, like your attorney profile page, and then leave, you may have an issue on that page that needs to be fixed, such as bad copy, bad graphics or long load time. If you find that people navigate to your contact page and then exit, that can be assumed as normal human behavior, and there is no issue present.

4. **Traffic source:** From where and how people get to your website. This is crucial to understanding what websites are driving your traffic. Are people coming from LinkedIn, Google or Twitter? This information helps you know where to focus your energy.

Of course, there is a lot more data on the Google Analytics tool that is very useful. These are simply the top four places to get started. If you can master these four areas of your web presence, you will be way ahead of your competition. These areas of analytics will arm you with the information you need to make educated decisions about where to spend your time and money as well as what needs to be fixed (if anything).

We mentioned above that having different phone numbers for each ad as a good practice; even that is more easily tracked online. There are services online that allow you to create unique numbers that all forward to your actual phone number; the only difference is that the call statistics are online, and you can see at a glance how many calls each number received. This isn't to say you have to get rid of your current phone number: in fact, you shouldn't. These numbers are only forwarding numbers and nothing more; clients with your old number can still get through perfectly fine.

The only application for tracking numbers is either a paid advertisement or a promotional piece that is used online. Remember that you should never use a tracking number on your website or any directory services.

In addition to Google Analytics, another great tool is Google Webmaster Tools, specifically because it tells you how many people are linking to you across the Internet and thus tells you how well your Internet marketing strategy is doing overall. This should be complemented by statistics on your email funnel and auto-responders, which should track how many people are getting and opening your emails.

On top of all that, there's your own internal CRM (Customer Relationship Management system): how much money you're charging, how long you're working, how long you spend with each client, etc. As we'll see, a CRM is an incredibly key resource in determining your ROI.

On that note, we're assuming that you already have an internal CRM in place. Discussing the process and tools to manage internal CRM is beyond the scope of this book, and there are many resources available to provide you with help and support when implementing your own CRM. It's a vital step in the tracking chain, and you need to have one before you can accurately calculate your ROI.

There are an almost unlimited number of things you can track online in order to measure your ROI, and if you're going to take anything away from this section, it should be this: it's imperative that you have a strong, stable, well-defined system in place to correctly track your ROI. Most of the clients we work with believe they have a process in place, but when it's subjected to a rigorous examination, it turns out that it breaks down. It's a good step that they even have a system in place, as it's good sense and a standard marketing practice: they're spending money, and they want to know where that money's going and how that money's helping them. For an Internet marketing strategy, however, you need to go above and beyond: you need to be taking in the data that show you the point of entry for all your clients.

An example monthly run-down of traffic data might look something like this: in total, 167 people visited our site this month. Of those visits, 35 came from Twitter, 120 from Google+ Local organic search and 12 from Facebook fan pages. Of these 167 visits, we collected 4 phone numbers, 5 appointment requests and 12 email addresses. We followed up with all of them; of the clients we followed up with, we closed 4, and each of them was worth $3200, on average. Last month, we had a net gain of $12,800 from our online activity.

This is very basic, and the numbers are simply examples, but it should give you an idea of how you should be looking at and tracking your Internet marketing strategy. This allows you to really get an accurate sense of valuation from clients that find you online: are they worth the same as clients who found you by driving by your office or from referral? We want to make sure you're capturing ROI information from those clients online, and these are extremely important statistics to know. Very often, we end up having to build new systems and processes for clients to get this reporting to be accurate. Make absolutely sure, when planning out your overall Internet marketing strategy, that you decide what metrics you're going to use and exactly how you're going to track them!

We can't stress this point enough: it's vital that you have a clear picture of your ROI online at all times. Efficient and accurate monitoring in this realm gives you an unparalleled advantage over traditional media: you can know, down to the dollar, whether spending in the online arena is good for your ROI. In fact, we tell most of our clients that if they're not getting at least three times their ROI on their Internet marketing, something is really wrong. Usually, it's more than that; three times the ROI is our bare minimum for clients to see. If you're not getting that, you need to go back and take a second look at your strategy. Either you've missed something along the way or you're in a really competitive market, and you need to bring in a second opinion or another expert to help you break into the market.

This does not happen in the first month. Getting to a position where you are ranked and your site is fully optimized for both search and conversion takes at least 6–9 months. Your overall strategy should focus on a multi-year approach. For example, in year one, we invested $35,000 in our web presence, and in year two and three, we focused on content and maintenance investing, at $21,000 per year. Over three years, our web strategy netted 94 new clients with a lifetime value of $3,200 each, for a total of $300,800 in net revenue. Each new client, on average, results in .25 of a referral, equaling an additional 23 clients. This brings our total net revenue from online activity plus the additional business that was generated to a grand total of $374,400. If you had an ATM where every time you inserted $5, it spit out $20, you would just stand there and keep inserting money. Your online presence is the same way: you have to keep at it.

Tracking your own ROI also gives you another advantage: should you choose to hire a firm to do this for you, you can tell whether or not the firm you hired is working well or not, and you can know whether you should stick with them or find someone new.

YOU'RE WORKING *with a firm, you should absolutely require them to provide you with these ROI reports. They can get them, and if they're not giving them to you or claim they're unable to get them, there's something seriously wrong: they're either hiding something or they're simply not as good as you thought they were!*

What this report needs to cover is how much traction your web presence is producing. Some numbers that you should follow include: website traffic, Google+ Local impressions, actions on Google+ Local, number of email addresses you received and number of people that requested appointments.

Your firm will be responsible for figuring out how many people are calling you because of your website. Put into place (an Excel spreadsheet should work fine) a system where, any time someone answers the phone and it is a new prospect, they are asked if they came from the web and where on the web they found you (Google+ Local, Yelp, AVVO, Google). This is the best way to track phone calls from the web. Obviously, it is not completely accurate, but remember that we can't use tracking numbers, so this is the best solution for now.

- You should be tracking your ROI (return on investment) for your Internet marketing so that you know if the money you're investing is actually working for you! Tracking this lets you know how well your online presence is working as well as what issues need to be fixed, if any.

- Internet marketing has an advantage over traditional advertising (such as through radio and TV) because its ROI can be much more easily tracked.

- You should be receiving three times your ROI from your Internet marketing efforts, at the minimum!

- Google Analytics and Google Webmaster Tools are both must-haves for your website! Using these tools, you will be able to track metrics like visitors' time on site, number of visitors, pages visited, keywords used by visitors, traffic sources, and how well your online presence is doing overall.

- In addition to statistics on your website, you should also have statistics on your auto-responders: how many people receive and open your emails.

- You must have a working internal Customer Resource Management system in place (measuring how much you charge, how much time you spend on each client's case, etc.) before you can accurately measure your ROI.

- If you choose to work with an agency for your Internet marketing, they should be able to give you a report of your ROI. If they won't—or can't—something is very wrong!

- Your online presence will take at least 6-9 months to get you where you want to be in terms of ranking and conversion. Successful Internet marketing takes time and is something you have to keep at!

Notes

CHAPTER 12

Reputation Defense

A Good Offense Is the Best Defense

As an attorney, your professional reputation is a huge part to your overall success and career. The truth about the Internet is that anyone, anonymously, can post anything they want to about you. From blog posts, online reviews, websites, to social media, there is a swath of opportunity for people to talk about you. In some cases, this is a positive thing, such as in online reviews from happy clients. In others, this can be extremely damaging and cause you to lose clients.

The first step to managing your reputation online is being aware of what is currently out there about you, your firm and your partners. With Google, you are able to search for phrases with quotations and get returns that must include every word in the search term. For example, you can type into the search box your name in quotes, and it will show you every website that has your name on it. (Try typing in your name with and without your middle initial.) Now, go through the first 30 pages of Google or so, and look for anything about you. Click on each page with mention of your name, and read what it says. We will get to what you can do in a moment.

For some people, this is difficult because you may have a common name. Only after you try to search with your name alone, go ahead and add the word "attorney" or "scam" after your search phrase like this: "Joe Smith" Attorney or "Joe Smith" scam

The words you want to be on the lookout for include scam, alert, ripoff, bad, rude, worst, never, etc.

The next thing you should do is set up a "Google Alert." Google Alert acts as notices or alerts and emails you any information you have requested that shows up in search. You add "your name," and every time your name appears online, Google will email you the websites that mention you. This is a crucial tool to managing your overall online presence, keeping you up to speed on who is talking about you. It is a great idea to set up a Google Alert for your name, firm name, partners and any products specific to your firm. This is a great tool for monitoring your reputation. If someone leaves a negative review about you online, you will be aware of that review and thus can take appropriate action.

Remember that very, very few people even visit the second page of Google, let alone the third or fourth. If you find something negative about you or your firm on the 16th page of Google, you may want to just leave it alone because no one is going to find it, anyway. Acting on something that is buried deep in search results can bring it to life and cause it to rise in the rankings, something you want to avoid at all cost. But sometimes, you need to act.

What do you do if you find something about you that is totally false and damaging to your reputation?

You are an attorney; send them a nasty gram telling them to take the information down. If their contact information is not readily available, you may be able to find them by entering their website URL into the whois.net search (**http://whois.net**). You do not need to threaten them, but you should be firm and brief. Usually, just asking someone to pull something down is enough. If you have to, take further action, depending on the specifics of the situation.

What to do if you find something about you that is true and damaging to your reputation?

This is going to happen. Someone is going to be angry about how things ended up, and they will take this rant online. You'll need to be prepared for this and calm down when you see it. It is difficult not to take this sort of thing personally, and in most respects, it is personal, but you want to act with a cool head. The first step is to see if you are in a place to respond to the comment. Some websites will allow you to comment, and some situations will warrant a reply. Do not get defensive: think about your reply carefully, and craft it as if a new prospect were reading both the complaint and your response. Do you come across as suspect in your reply? If so, re-write it, and maybe even have someone you trust read it before submitting it.

At times like this, it might be a good idea to take a look at yourself or your firm. If the complaint is truly justified, take this as a learning moment, and make the appropriate adjustments. This takes more courage than just sweeping it under the rug. Truly great attorneys know when they could've done something better and will make the right adjustments to avoid future mistakes. Be one of those attorneys.

Managing Negative Remarks That Are Ranking High in Search:

The title of this chapter says it all: a good offense is definitely better than a good defense. Since we know that few people navigate to page two and beyond of search results, we are going to use that to our advantage. Thus, our end goal is not to remove or react to the negative content but to push it so far down in search results that no normal person will ever find it.

Your targeted goal is about 20 unique websites that you control with your inputted content, which you want to rank above the negative website(s). Here is a list of the best places to start (hint: a lot of these websites will rank high without you doing anything):

1. Your own website

2. Google+

3. Facebook

4. LinkedIn

5. Twitter

6. Quora

7. About.me

8. Avvo

9. Yelp

10. Merchant Circle

11. Amazon

12. Personal website just about you

13. Pinterest

14. Better Business Bureau

15. Chamber of Commerce

16. Local Bar Association

17. National Bar Association

18. Press Releases

19. Blogs

20. Videos

In the main search area—where all the links appear on Google—if you set up your website correctly, Google will allow you to have up to four links on the first page all from your own website, with subpages and subdomains. Be sure to set up your website so that you get the full extent of this opportunity.

With complete and active accounts on all these sites, you can ensure that any negative information will be pushed to the third page or farther down; this is usually more than enough to solve any issue. Sometimes, people get really pissed off, and they may write things that are far too harsh, such as "Joe Smith is a Scam Artist". If you are dealing with a situation where someone has flat-out called you a scam artist, you should include some posts on the above sites that talk about "scams" or "ripoffs" to help those sites outrank the negative comments.

We hope you never have to deal with this kind of issue, but you are dealing with clients that sometimes have very difficult, emotional circumstances that may ensnare you. If you can, it is occasionally helpful to call the person who posted and talk to them about the issue. You can always politely ask them to take down the comment, and see what happens.

Managing Negative Reviews:

From time to time, someone is going to give you a negative review on Google+ Local or another directory website. Don't raise the alarm; just respond by getting more positive reviews than negative reviews. If you get a negative review, immediately reach out to a few clients, and ask them personally to review your firm at that same website.

The truth of the matter is that having some negative reviews on directory sites can actually be a good thing. This may sound counterintuitive, but think about human behavior: if people think something appears too positive, they may wonder if they are being gamed with regard to your online presence. They may ask themselves, "Did this attorney write all these good reviews?" Having a healthy blend of reviews with a few negative ones will make you look more human and more appealing to prospects. Odds are, not everyone would give you a perfect 10, even if you were doing your job to the best of your ability.

- As an attorney, your professional reputation is extremely important to your career, which means that you must manage your online reputation.

- On the Internet, anyone can anonymously post anything they want about you. Sometimes, this is a good thing, such as when happy clients leave good reviews. Other times, you'll have to deal with negative comments.

- To manage your online reputation, you need to know what is being said about you online. To find out, do several searches for your name in quotation marks, followed by your name and the words attorney, scam, ripoff, etc. Set up a Google Alert to let you know when and where people are talking about you.

- If you find a negative comment that is false and damaging, you may want to ask the commenter to take it down. If you find a negative comment that is substantiated, you may want to calmly reply in order to fix the situation.

- If you find negative reviews that rank high in search results, don't worry: all is not lost! Aim to have around 20 websites, with positive content you control, rank for your name and firm name, including your own website, Facebook, AVVO, Yelp, etc. These websites should bury the negative reviews where no one will find them in search results.

- Remember that few people visit the second page of Google—and even fewer visit the pages after that. It may not be necessary to act upon negative comments or reviews that are already buried in search results.

- Also remember that a mix of good and bad reviews can be a good thing! While you want mostly good reviews, a bad review or two can assure skeptical people that your good reviews are honest, not a scam.

CHAPTER 13

Mobile:

All Things Mobile Search and Mobile Websites

During our CLE events, attorneys are always asking us if real clients actually use mobile devices to search for law firms online. This is a very valid concern because you do not want to focus time and energy on something that isn't being used.

By the Numbers:

Over the last year, we have tracked traffic to our clients' websites, accounting for tens of thousands of clicks. We also collaborated with a competitor that provides web services to attorneys, and they corroborated our data. As it turns out, almost 19% of all traffic to attorneys' websites originates from mobile phones. That's nearly 1 in 5!

We've held this particular topic to the very end, but this is perhaps the most immediate of all the upcoming challenges in Internet marketing. Mobile devices are rapidly becoming the primary mode of interaction with the Internet; Mary Meeker of Morgan-Stanley has recently estimated that, given current mobile trends, the number of mobile devices that connect to the Internet will eclipse that of regular desktop PCs and laptops by mid-2013. You heard that right: by 2014, more people will be connecting to the Internet by phone than by computer.

In fact, mobile is already a driving force behind many of the search engine changes we've seen. Google is setting up its local search infrastructure so that there is an improved focus on mobile because it believes users will continue to increase their search behavior on mobile. Mobile search is a different creature than traditional search and requires a different approach.

Users who search mobile used to be driven by the "I need something right now that's near me" mentality, as opposed to a more research-oriented desktop user who is more willing to sift through answers and Wikipedia articles. Very few people were willing to do that on a mobile phone; most likely, they were looking for a business nearby they could walk or drive to quickly. Now, that mentality is changing.

More and more, as people are out to lunch, driving around or talking, they're thinking to themselves: "Oh! I'll just use my phone really quick to search for an answer." The same applies to sitting around, eating dinner or watching TV at home: chances are, they have their iPhone, Android phone or tablet sitting right next to them. Instead of waiting to look up the answer to their problem on their computer, they'll just pick up their mobile device and look up the answer right then and there.

This is great news, even for attorneys (although many attorneys have looked skeptically at us when we've said this). The fact that the mobile search mentality has changed to include more research-oriented problem solving means that you can now get in the mobile search game and expand your website's reach.

This might seem far-fetched, but it's actually not: think about your own mobile smartphone use or the usage patterns you've observed in others. There's a clear aura of instant gratification with any sort of mobile device, and users take advantage of this to get an immediate answer.

If your site is not mobile-friendly or your Google+ Local page is non-existent (Google+ Local is extremely mobile-friendly), you're going to get left out in the cold when it comes to getting prospects on mobile.

Remember when we said that mobile search is a different animal and requires a different approach? Because of space constraints, the mobile realm tightens up the ranking requirements quite a bit. On regular desktop Internet, you've got to be in the top 7 rankings; it's great to be in the top 3 or 4, but 7's the bare minimum. On mobile devices, if you're not in the top 2, you're not being seen: very few people scroll down on mobile phones, and often, they simply tap the first or second result they see. This is important to you because mobile phones offer an unparalleled ease of use; for example, many phones, like iPhone and Android, offer built-in calling from the web.

Users can simply tap a finger on your phone number, and the smart-phone dials the number automatically, without any need to pick up another phone. As mobile devices become more and more common, it's of critical importance that your site is mobile-friendly and sits in that A or B listing of Google's returns so that it's seen by as many prospects as possible. (FIGURE 27)

FIGURE 27. MOBILE SEARCH SCREEN

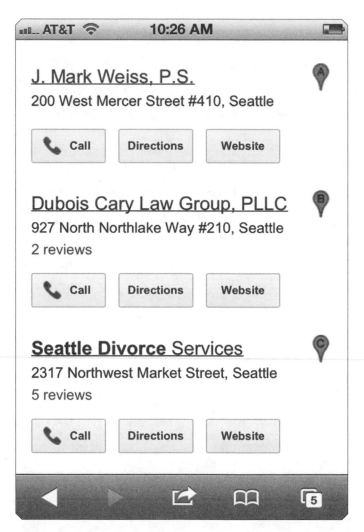

There is no question that the number of people using mobile is only going to rise, so yes, this is very important. And since mobile is only going to increase in importance, you should start thinking about mobile and what separates it from other search. The two biggest areas that you must focus on are mobile search and how your website looks on a mobile device.

Mobile Search:

The two biggest players in mobile operating systems are Apple (iPhone) and Android (pretty much everyone else). Until recently, these two systems shared most of their search and map functions with the same online reference centers. This meant that a user searching on an Android phone would be getting the same results as a person with an iPhone. Well, all of that has changed, and with that, you need to have knowledge of and a strategy for two separate operating systems. It's important to note that Android users have eclipsed iPhone users in the U.S. in 2011. http://techcrunch.com/2011/01/06/android-passes-iphone/

So, how do you get ranked on a mobile phone?

Apple (iPhone):

In July, Apple announced the launch of iOS 6, which launched in the fall of 2012. The update to Apple's mobile operating system (for the iPhone, iPad and iPod Touch) introduces several interesting changes to the way mobile search currently operates.

In the most stunning change, Apple broke away from Google Maps entirely, creating its own Maps app (mostly powered by

Tom-Tom and Yelp) that features local search with "Info Cards," navigation with turn-by-turn directions (spoken by Siri), interactive 3D views and Siri integration. (Before this change, Apple was using Google Maps integrated with Siri.)

In the new Maps, the user can type in a local search or can ask Siri to do a local search for them. On the results page, the user can see the result or tap a pin on the map to see the business' "Info Card." This Info Card will have the name, address, phone number and website (if there is one) of the business. On the card will also be local business ratings and reviews from Yelp as well as photos and deals.

While Apple has not officially disclosed the directories that they are using to populate their business listings, their copyright page acknowledges Acxiom and Localeze (http://gspsa21.ls.apple.com/html/attribution.html). According to Apple's iOS 6 presentation by Scott Forstall, Apple "has already ingested more than 100 million business listings around the world" for their local search.

Now is the time to start starting caring about these changes (and about mobile search, if you don't already). It would be very unwise to ignore this new development from Apple: millions of people in the U.S. (and around the world) use iPhones. (In 2012 alone, Apple sold 68,544,000 iPhones, according to data from Apple reports.) And now, iPhone users can utilize Maps to do local search and even get turn-by-turn directions to every search result, bypassing Google completely.

To prepare for and compete in this new game, you'll have to make sure that your business is listed correctly on Acxiom, Localeze and Yelp. This is just to start since no one knows yet if these data providers are the exclusive providers for Maps. If your business is listed incorrectly (or worse, not listed at all), you could lose out on a portion of potential business by not showing up in the search results of Apple Maps.

In addition, you should be adding photos to your listings and working to encourage happy clients to leave positive reviews on Yelp (which we covered in an earlier chapter) since these reviews will now be an integral part of Maps and may play a part in where your business is ranked in Apple's search results. Photos and reviews will also make your Info Card more attractive to potential customers. (This is true not only of Maps but of Google+ Local as well.)

Getting Ranked on Android:

So, even though Apple's release of Maps changes the game a little bit, that doesn't mean that you can abandon Google. Android has more users than iPhone and is still powered by Google. All the same rules apply for Android and Google: if you follow the previous chapters on getting ranked locally and using the right type of SEO for your website, you are already 90% of the way to getting ranked highly on an Android device. The only addition you need to make to round out your mobile search efforts is focusing on Yelp and Localeze to include Apple.

By focusing on Yelp and especially Localeze, you will be ensuring that you have created the appropriate local directories for Android (and most of iPhone as well).

We know with 100% certainty that mobile marketing will change within the next twelve months.

As the mobile local search game continues to progress, check back with us:

http://www.GetNoticedGetFound.com/mobile

Creating a Mobile-Ready Website:

Your mobile-ready website needs to be easy to read, navigate and use. Not so easy on such a tiny screen, compared to a 15-inch monitor. The biggest killer for conversion on mobile is having a site that the user can't see or use.

Think about it: have you ever visited a website on your phone and couldn't read any of the text because the words were too tiny and impossible to see? Or worse, the site didn't pull up at all? We have seen everything, from websites that look terrible to websites where you can't click on the phone number to call the person or business (another killer of mobile websites).

In the development world both tablets and mobile devices are considered mobile. For some sites, the website design from the desktop is suitable for a tablet or iPad. Take this example: (when used on an iPad this website is easy to read and navigate) (FIGURE 28)

FIGURE 28. BRANTON IPAD WEBSITE

When it comes to preparing your website for mobile, there are two main options for law firms:

1. Responsive Websites

2. Mobile-Friendly Websites

Responsive Websites:

A responsive website auto-adjusts the layout and copy on the website to match the size of the screen available. If you view a responsive website on a mobile phone, it will be in one long column with big buttons. Look at that same website on a tablet or laptop, and the site may be three columns with regular-sized buttons.

Creating a responsive website requires certain coding to be put into place in the architecture of your website. For most attorneys, this is not something you will be implementing yourself. Asking your Webmaster to handle this is the most advised strategy for creating a responsive website.

One disadvantage to responsive websites is that you are unable to organize your content for ideal optimization on a mobile device while maintaining ideal optimization of your website when it is viewed from a desktop. This snafu is caused by the nature of how a responsive website compresses your website layout.

Some advantages of responsive websites include ease of updating and having one solution that encompasses mobile, tablet (iPad) and desktop compatibility. Since a responsive site is just a compression of your current site, any changes you make to the website are automatically added to the mobile version. Thus, you only need one type of solution, as opposed to three separate solutions.

Mobile-Friendly Websites:

The second option is to create a separate website specific to mobile, with a unique layout when compared to your website viewed on a desktop. This site is separate from your regular website. When a user attempts to navigate to your website on their mobile device, they are automatically re-directed to the mobile-friendly version (sometimes denoted by a **m.url.com**).

These sites are best optimized for conversion on mobile. Even though complete testing has not definitively proven the conversion rates between responsive websites and mobile-friendly websites, you are able to control exactly what the user sees on a mobile-friendly website without altering your main website. That means you are in complete control of the conversion strategy on both websites, compared to a responsive website that compresses content beyond your control.

The key components that you should implement in your mobile-friendly website are a tiled design (see below), access to the right information in one click and easy contact options. (FIGURE 29)

To achieve this, we recommend you have a "call us" and "email us" button on your main mobile-friendly website. Then, make sure that a prospect can access your attorney profile page, map, services and blog.

The biggest disadvantage to a mobile-friendly website is you are likely to lose real estate for copy in exchange for ease of navigation.

FIGURE 29. BRANTON MOBILE FRIENDLY WEBSITE

By having large, easy to navigate buttons on your home page, you will be pushing copy down below the screen. The user will have to scroll down to read the content.

Whichever type of mobile website you choose, it is important that you choose one. This is traffic that you can't afford to miss. Poorly designed mobile sites will both convert less and perform poorly from an SEO perspective.

To assist with your conversions, a great branding strategy will help you communicate clearly to the user what and who you are, even on a mobile device.

The important thing to remember about mobile is that the mobile search user is a fast-growing segment of the population. Don't miss out on almost 20% of leads just because you don't have a mobile website and strategy!

- Mobile users now account for 19%, nearly 1 in 5, of traffic to attorney websites! This number is only growing, as more and more people connect to the Internet on mobile phones.

- If your website is impossible to read—or worse—doesn't load on a mobile phone, you'll miss out on a large number of potential clients. To reach these leads, you must have a mobile-ready website.

- The two biggest killers of mobile conversions are a website that is hard to read and navigate on a mobile device and a phone number on the website that can't be clicked on to call.

- Mobile search requires a different approach than desktop search; the screen is much smaller, showing fewer results for a search. While you can be in the top 7 in search results on a desktop, you must be in the top two on a mobile phone: any lower, and you won't be seen on the screen unless the user scrolls down (and most people don't).

- Apple and Android are the two biggest players in mobile, so you want to rank highly on both. To rank on Android, just continue your efforts to rank on Google (Android is powered by Google). Because Apple's Maps feature is no longer powered by Google, you need to add a few extra things to rank on Apple: make sure you're listed correctly on Yelp and Localeze.

- There are two options for creating a mobile-ready website: a responsive website, which is your main website with coding included to compress it when viewed on a mobile device, or a mobile website, which is a separate website just for mobile devices.

- Responsive and mobile websites each have their advantages and disadvantages, so you'll have to decide which one will work best for your Internet strategy. Whichever you choose, you must choose one!

What's Next

If you've reached this chapter, give yourself a pat on the back: you've done more for your online Internet marketing strategy than many local businesses will ever do.

That's no reason to get complacent, however: the Internet is, by its very nature, a fast-moving target. Internet marketing isn't going to stay in stasis, and you'll have to work to keep up with it. With that in mind, this chapter is dedicated to what's coming down the road: things that aren't yet a major player in online marketing but absolutely will be in the near future. These are things that a local business has to think about and look toward: new technologies and trends that will have to be incorporated into your marketing strategy in order to keep at the top of your game.

Social

We've obviously covered a great deal of social media previously, and you're well equipped to handle the social network scene at the moment. What we didn't cover, however, is the future of social networks: how they're going to change and how that's going to impact your overall online marketing strategy.

The first and most important aspect of future social is this: eventually, social media services are going to be more than just places where people connect. In the future, social media networks are going to transform into something more search engine-oriented; people will go to Facebook not just to interact but to search for things as well. This makes it crucial that you have an established presence early on. It is not too late, and you are not far behind the curve: start now by creating presences on sites like LinkedIn, Twitter, Facebook, YouTube, Google+ and other social media sites. This doesn't mean you have to interact with all of these social media networks every day or even very frequently (though you'll want to keep in touch more often with the main ones, as per the social network chapter). What you do want, however, is a presence; at least make sure that your listings are, in fact, on these websites—you'll be very glad for it later.

Social networks are also getting very location-oriented as time progresses, so we can expect that trend to continue; this will eventually lead to a sort of social-mobile combo: users who are searching while also in their Facebook mobile app. This is already a pattern that exists, and we've noticed a rise in this user behavior recently. It's actually quite common now. Users are in the Facebook app and simply go to a Facebook Places listing to see what's around them. Your first reaction might be that this makes the most sense for restaurants and bars (and they've already start to capitalize on the opportunity), but this is useful for firms as well. Facebook users will note, "Oh, this is where so-and-so's office is," and they'll remember it. You need to have this local presence because if you're not there, and you're not found, someone else will be.

This social / search hybrid that we're seeing slowly creep into existence will also form another important piece of Internet marketing going forward: a combination of social word-of-mouth and Google ranking. Instead of letting Google figure out who's first, more people are going to go on Facebook and see what their friends think. Your interaction level, reviews and presence on Facebook are going to be crucial at this stage of the game. More people are going to search there the way they're currently searching on Google. Some Internet results will still trickle through, but much of the results will come from the client's social networks.

This is important because people in general will take how their friends and family have viewed businesses very, very seriously: from a marketing perspective, it's a well-known and proven fact that people give far more weight to opinions from friends and family than from any other source of marketing. As a result, this combo of social search is going to be very influential, so you should keep an eye on it as it progresses.

Social Search

As seen on Law Practice Today:

http://www.americanbar.org/newsletter/publications/law_practice_today_home/law_practice_today_archive/june12/social-media-and-search-the-impending-marriage.html

You may have already seen social media posts appear when searching on Google or Bing and so have your potential clients. Once you understand the reason for social media's integration into search, you can begin building a strategy that will dramatically enhance your online presence, ultimately expanding your practice.

What is social search? It is a mix of search returns that include both websites, which are highly ranked, and suggestions from people within your social network.

Since we often prefer to get recommendations from other people, the blending of social and search makes perfect sense. We still ask our friends and family for suggestions on what doctors to see, attorneys to call and accountants to do our taxes. An obvious extension of this is asking for friends' opinions on Google, Yelp, Facebook, Avvo and other social websites.

Since 2008, we have seen a move from traditional search toward a blended search model that integrates both traditional search and your personal social network. For Google, this is called "Social Search." This integration links its social networking site Google+ into its search returns on Google. Bing and Yahoo have also been integrating social networks into search returns for years. It will not be long before we simply expect to see the integration of our social network in our search returns.

Mike Grehan, VP and Global Content Director of Incisive Media, publisher of Search Engine Watch and ClickZ and producer of the Search Engine Strategies international conference series says:

> End users who previously couldn't vote for content via links from web pages are now able to vote for content with their clicks, bookmarks, tags and ratings. These are very strong signals to search engines, and, best of all, they don't rely on the elitism of one website owner linking to another or the often mediocre crawl of a dumb bot.

Grehan, Mike, *New Signals To Search Engines* - http://www.acronym.com/new-signals-to-search-engines.html *(March 2009).*

> This shift in the way we obtain referrals and the way search engines come up with results will have a profound impact on your law practice. This, along with local search, is an enormous opportunity for law firms. When alerted of a major shift in how future clients will find businesses, it's wise to take note.

> To be competitive, you need to create a strategy for both social and search. SEO and an online presence are still undoubtedly relevant; however, social media has become an integral part of a successful online strategy.

> SEO and your overall online presence will maintain a central role in your firm's online strategy; however, adding a well-planned social campaign will do even more to cement your

place online for years to come. What this means for your firm is simple: in order to maintain online search ranking and increased conversions, your next step is to integrate a social media campaign centered on your prospects.

When delivering technology CLE's, I am regularly asked to identify which social media sites law firms should focus on. The quick answer is that law firms should concentrate on several. Adding multiple social networks to your online arsenal will both increase your online exposure and mitigate the risk that a Google algorithm update may negatively impact your SEO strategy.

The following is a breakdown of the different major social networking sites and the components that you should focus on within each site:

Twitter

After July 2nd, 2011, following a failure to renew an agreement, Tweets (updates) no longer appeared directly in Google search returns; however, an experiment done by Rand Fishkin, CEO of SEOMoz, tells us that Google is still using Twitter aggregators and scrappers to bring the billions of posts on Twitter into the influence of the search rankings. The amount of Re-Tweets by your firm's followers has a large impact on the influence of a Tweet. Also of importance is the

"Title Tag" of the links you are trying to support by tweeting them. (The Title Tag is the description you give a website that can appear on links.)

Facebook

Although not completely indexed by Google, this site is still the 800-pound gorilla of social networks. People spend more time on Facebook than any other social media site. Pages (your firm's Page, not your personal Page) are indexed by Google, as are the comments made on third party sites. Bing and other networks are indexing "likes." You should focus on integrating your blog onto your Page as well as boosting your "likes." Adding a Facebook social plugin to your website's blog would also be beneficial.

Linkedin

This social network's users have the highest median income and aren't afraid to discuss business. You can and should create a business page for your firm. Connect your blog and your Twitter stream to the LinkedIn update stream. With their recent change— allowing groups to be "open" (public)—you are best suited to focus on two areas: LinkedIn Groups and your Personal Profile. Optimize your profile with your keywords and geo-location. Join groups where your prospects are likely to be located, and add genuine, valuable and useful content in the discussion stream.

Google Plus (g+)

With Google+, there is seamless integration into their search platform. Establishing a business page and creating a description will allow someone searching within your practice area to easily find you. To attract readership, you should follow people within your industry and pay attention to the people that interact with them. There is also value to the +1 button that Google allows you to add to your website. Similar to the "like" button from Facebook, this is an easy tool for readers of your blog to send a positive search signal to Google.

As an attorney, you have a responsibility both to practice law and also to build your practice. Adding a social media strategy is an opportunity to expand your practice's reach, establish a strong foundation online and preserve your legacy. You will need an SEO plan, a properly designed website, local directory listings and a blog. With the proper web presence to support a social campaign, you will see rapid results. Combine all this with a social strategy, and you won't know what to do with all the business.

As you can see, there is a connection and merging of social and search. It has not been fully fleshed out, but this is something that is coming soon.

A Special Tool for Your Office
Save time with a ScanSnap Fujitsu desk scanner

Even though this book is about creating your online presence, part of this presence necessarily involves paper documents. When we find something to help our attorney clients that works great and saves us time, we want to share that information.

To put it simply – the ScanSnap scanner is amazing. One of the first things we noticed about the scanner is how fast it scans documents. Just for fun, we loaded the scanner with about 18 pages of documents and hit the button. In a flash, page after page zipped through the scanner, and the documents began to appear on our computer screen. The outstanding thing is that the scanner manages multiple sizes of documents, both front and back, without any extra effort.

At our office, we use this to scan agreements and letters from attorneys and bar associations, along with anything else we need to add to our archives. Since we operate on the cloud, we are able to easily add documents to our shared folders and access that information later.

As we travel the country delivering CLE's about technology, we hear a lot of conversations from attorneys about finding technology that makes life easier and saves them time. ScanSnap is one of those technologies.

Even if you are not migrating to the cloud yet, this device helps you keep every document on your computer for easy access. With integration into certain CRM software, ScanSnap can sometimes upload those documents directly to clients' files.

I spoke with the Product Manager from ScanSnap to find out a little more about what they have planned.

Michael Sidejas – Product Manager Fujitsu

What separates ScanSnap from other similar products?

Fujitsu has been making scanners for over two decades. Over the course of the last 7–10 years, things have been changing. You might have noticed that scanners are getting much smaller. Not only did scanners get smaller, the people that are using them are changing. It is no longer just people scanning that are professionals; it is people using the document scanner to archive, scan and preserve information.

The whole premise of the ScanSnap technology is that it is easy to use. We have taken the complication out of imaging and made it simple. As we get more into cloud services, and people realize they are being laden with paper, that is when a scanner becomes important to them. We want everyone to know that when they put the paper in and push that button, exactly what they think is going to happen is delivered. There are so many technologies out there that just don't do that. We want people to know that the experience is all about the user's experience and drive to meet their expectations.

Where is the world of ScanSnap going, or scanning in general?

The next big step is going to [be] scanning directly into the cloud services. And it's going to continue to be that way as people consolidate. Either through cloud services provided by a third party or even a step to people creating their own personal clouds. That is where we are headed with ScanSnap. I know from my personal use that I am using mobile technology and smart phone technology to share and collaborate and to become accessible to content. Cloud service is very popular among the Mac community. They are bypassing other services and going straight to cloud services. When it comes down to why you move into a scan environment, sometimes it is to unclutter your documents. Having those documents available on the cloud helps you collaborate with content.

What can the Attorneys expect from ScanSnap in the future?

A lot of product development comes right out of customer feedback. There is a tremendous amount of cohesion inside our department. Our marketing and customer call support center are in the building. This provides great statistical data for user requests. When the customer support department says, "Hey, we are getting a lot of people asking to scan images into different programs." We are able to notice when we have, say, 8 percent of users requesting a specific function. We live in a compressed society, our music is compressed, our videos are compressed, and we figured out that we could add the option to push a button and have a compressed scanned image go directly into [Adobe] Photoshop. In the future, we look for the number of calls for features and use that information to decide when we should put something as a direct function of the ScanSnap. We use customer feedback to make those decisions.

Direct Mailing To Online Source

You may wonder why we're putting direct mailing in the "What's Next" category; after all, in Internet marketing terms, direct mailing is older than dust. It's here because there's definite potential for it as the years roll on. Like fashion from the seventies becoming popular again, direct mailing is making a small comeback. The reason for this is partly because of its scarcity. Sending mail every now and then, done properly, is not a poor marketing option. It's not something you should rely on heavily, but it's definitely something to keep in your arsenal to use where it's appropriate.

If you already have a direct mail campaign going and want to keep doing it, you need to find a way to incorporate Google+ Local, Facebook, your website or a call to action in your direct mailers: you have to shift the goal to getting people online. Direct mailing with mobile is an especially attractive option; being able to snap a picture and go straight to a website to see information or reviews or being able to text a certain number to get a special report are options that look very promising.

Texting

As mentioned with direct mailing, you can now have people text a number to receive information; they're actually entering your marketing funnel the moment they text that number. This is all automatic. You can have the same auto-responder system set up so that it sends texts in the same way that it sends emails. If a user puts in their mobile phone number, they could get a text that says something like: "We've received your name and email. Thank you very much for getting in contact! Check your email for a special report, free of charge. One of our representatives will be in touch!"

There is one other aspect about texting that should be mentioned here: some in the restaurant / bar business have automatic texts that send the latest coupons or deals, like Tuesday Happy Hours, Five for Four Fridays—marketing ploys like that. It's very common in the restaurant / bar scene, but we've only started to implement some of those ideas with our attorney clients. This could be taken as spammy by some; depending on your niche, this might work for you. Make sure to visit our blog **http://www.GetNoticedGetFound.com/blog** to stay up-to-date with our research in this area.

Once a prospect gives out their mobile phone number, don't be afraid to send out texts once or twice a month. Make sure the texts are useful, and don't send them more than once or twice per month: that could start to seem spammy. Texts are read over 90% of the time once received, as opposed to emails, which are read only 17-20% of the time (and those are optimistic numbers). A well-placed, well-timed text or two every now and then can really help drum up business and get some clients to call you.

Direct Voicemail

Direct voicemail is the practice of sending a voicemail directly to the phone without the phone ever ringing. This is now possible to do with mobile phone voicemail systems, and, in actuality, it works very well. These systems are quite nifty. You can set up outbound voicemails that talk about something new or something local that you and your firm did. The voicemail can be about 30 to 90 seconds, and, instead of calling, you can send it directly to their phone. The users are notified that there is a voicemail, but the phone never rings, meaning they can see the voicemail message and listen whenever they want. It's non-intrusive, and the listen rate is much higher as a result.

This is one of the reasons we recommended earlier to get mobile phone numbers from your leads; it not only opens up the texting avenue but the direct voicemail avenue as well. Direct voicemail is very personal and very effective, and it's best used for events or other local things your firm might be doing. If your firm does seminars in your practice area, dropping a direct voicemail to each of your clients is a great, personal way to let them know about your upcoming seminars.

Summing Up

We called this chapter the "What's Next" chapter for a reason: many of these technologies are going to affect the Internet marketing arena. In fact, some of these ideas and strategies that we've talked about are already coming into play. We've begun to experiment with these things with some of our clients who are ahead of the curve or are battling in very competitive markets, which illustrates that these ideas are not simply theory or fluff. They're real strategies that are beginning to come into the market, and it's a good idea to keep abreast of them going forward.

Talk to an agency that you're working with, and see what their ideas are on these future strategies. Nothing's set in stone with them, and a creative idea or two could really put you ahead in these areas. It's also important that you find the right agency—one who specializes in these techniques: these aren't things your average webmaster will know how to do, and chances are, an average webmaster hasn't even heard of them. Make sure you talk to an agency or service that thoroughly understands the full realm of Internet marketing, how it works with other marketing and has knowledge of future strategies down the line.

- You're already way ahead of many local businesses by making it this far. But that doesn't mean you can rest on your laurels. The Internet is *constantly* changing, so you need to keep up!

- Social media will eventually transform into a social search hybrid, where people go to search and ask for recommendations as well. (In fact, we're seeing the beginnings of this already.) Social will also become increasingly location-oriented. Focus on having a presence on Facebook, Twitter, LinkedIn and Google+ to get ahead of this curve.

- Direct mailing is making a comeback because of its current scarcity and should be used to direct prospective clients to your website.

- Texting can be a great marketing tool—you can have prospects text for information, such as a special report. When you get someone's mobile phone number, don't hesitate to send them a helpful text once or twice a month to increase your business. (Texts are read over 90% of the time when received!)

- Direct voicemail is a non-intrusive, personal way of reaching out to potential clients and increasing your business—let prospects know about local events you are involved in, seminars in your practice area, etc.

- Think about implementing these strategies to put yourself ahead of your competitors., and be creative! If you're working with an agency, make sure they know about upcoming changes in Internet marketing and how they can help your firm.

Notes

CHAPTER 15

How to Find People to Do This for You

T he last thing you're going to need is a workforce. Let's face it: you didn't go to law school, pass the bar and build up your practice just so you could spend 11 non-billable hours a day uploading videos, submitting listings to directories and designing websites.

Now, we really wish we had better news for you, but finding competent people to do this work for you is not easy. Most web designers are broke, they know nothing about marketing, and many don't have any clients outside of your local city. (And yes, they often live in their parents' basement.) That is not the kind of person you can trust with your marketing budget, so be thorough in deciding who to invest with.

We get asked all the time about where and how to find a good web person. And our answer is that every time we find one who knows what they are doing (they are rare), we hire them to work on our team.

Outsourcing this work to India or to some fly-by-night firm will cause more work than it will save. And having one of your clerks or assistants do this work will drive you both crazy and could irreversibly ruin your working relationship.

So, How Can I Get All of This Done?

First, local web marketing is probably the most time-sensitive, urgent issue on your practice calendar right now. It may not seem like it at the moment, but when you look back on this book 6-18 months from now, you will probably wish that you had a time machine to get you back to this day. The local Internet marketing door is WIDE open right now, but it is closing fast…and we would not want you to miss out on securing the financial future of your practice just because you had a big case load.

On the other hand, it's very difficult to find good people to help you with your online presence. Most web designers are flakes. Even if a web designer knows how to put up a good site, it doesn't mean they can get you on page #1 of Google. And outsourcing this kind of work to India or the Philippines is a waste of time and money. (We've tried it…and won't make that mistake again).

In the interest of full disclosure, we provide a turnkey, 100% Done-For-You service, which means you send us your business contact information, and we do the rest – All you do is approve the work before it goes live. It's literally ALL done for you. Plus, we know how to get results faster than anyone. Our services are on the expensive side: you will probably be able to find someone to do a bare-bones job for much less. But the way to look at it is this: we invest a lot of money into our client's future. And, when you get 3, 5 or 9 more clients a month at $5,000 or more, we all win.

We built our company on consulting with attorneys and providing them guidance on establishing a proper web presence. One of our founders, Jabez LeBret, used to work at Nordstrom. He brought with him the belief that you provide service to everyone, regardless of whether or not they are your customers. Sometimes you are not the right fit for us, and in those cases, we would love to recommend you to another firm.

We are restricting ourselves to only a handful of clients in any given geographical area. Your area may already be spoken for... and while that's not to say we won't take you, there's a good chance we will be committed already and have to pass.

If that is the case, we would love the opportunity to send you to a trusted resource and place where we know you are in good hands. Our goal above and beyond anything else is to make sure attorneys have the right information before they make a decision. Sometimes that right decision is us, and sometimes it is not.

Having said all of that, if you feel that you are a firm that we should choose to work with, and you would like to find out about our team's availability to help you get all of this DONE FOR YOU, please contact us at...

Phone: (513) 444-2016

Fax: 415-520-0332

Email: expert@GetNoticedGetFound.com

Web: http://www.GetNoticedGetFound.com

We will, at the very least, be able to tell you if we are already working with an attorney in your area.

If we decide to move forward with you, we always start with a Web Strategy Diagnosis. There is no obligation on either your or our part. This just begins the discussion regarding how we may be able to help you. And while we know that some people take this experience-backed, high-quality web strategy and then go and hire another firm, we also know that the best customers—those who understand the value of growing their business by maximizing their online marketing investment—will ask us, "Do it for me." We are looking for a small number of clients to build a long-term relationship with. And if that sounds like your firm, then please feel free to write or call.

With that, we bid you adieu. You've reached the end of this book, but you certainly haven't reached the end of how we can help you. If you've followed all the techniques and processes in this book and really took it to heart, you're very prepared to wade into the online marketing arena and come out the victor. You are ahead of most of your competitors, and you have a clear idea of what lies in store. Don't get complacent, be creative, and you'll be successful in the online marketing arena for many years to come!

Notes

Our CLE Program

How to Bring the Authors to Your Next Event

Topeka Bar Association
534 South Kansas Ave.,
Suite 1130,
Topeka, Kansas 66603
Telephone (785) 233-3945
www.topekabar.com

October 8, 2012
Mr. Jabez LeBret
Re: Presentation – Get Noticed, Get Found

Dear Jabez,

Thank you so much for coming to Topeka to present "Get Noticed, Get Found". You did an amazing job delivering your message and keeping everyone engaged. The program was very educational, enlightening and informative. The information offered could be used not only by law firms, but any business.

I really enjoyed getting to know you a little during your brief stay in Topeka. I must admit that I was a bit skeptical about your program. I thought it may be a way to promote your book. But, I was pleasantly surprised. You are truly interested in getting the best and latest information to the public. Plus, as a bonus, you are just a wonderful and genuinely nice person.

Many attendees responded with excellent evaluations. I would recommend the program to anyone that wants to market their firm and would be happy to visit with anyone interested in your presentation.

Please stop by again if you are in the area. All the best,

Paula Huff,
Executive Director
Topeka Bar Association
Topeka Kansas

How To Bring The Authors To Your Next Event or CLE:

For a certain number of CLE's we will waive our speaking fee and travel expenses as part of our book tour. To find out if your bas association fits our book tour schedule please contact us directly at:

Get Noticed Get Found

CLE Program

513.444.2016

or email

CLE@GetNoticedGetFound.com

Both Mark Homer and Jabez LeBret have delivered over a combined 1,100 presentations. In 2012 Get Noticed Get Found delivered over 45 CLE's and spoke and several State Bar Annual Events.

We offer three different CLE's and in most states these CLE's qualify for from 1.0 credits to 3.0 credits and can include an optional ethics credit.

Our CLE Programs:

"The attendance was excellent, and I was amazed to see the high quality of evaluations returned. Almost everyone gave both of you, the speakers, and the topic, a 5 out of a possible 5 score." **Peter Steiner, Executive Director Sonoma County Bar Association**

Our Program For Bar Associations and Legal Events

Tech Tips for Attorneys: Ethics and/or General Credit (Our most popular CLE)

Websites, Google, Email, Client Confidentiality, and More... Online Management: the Ethics, Pitfalls, & Techniques, from Social Media Traps to Disclaimers.

This 60 minute, 90 minute, or 1/2 day presentation qualifies in most states for 1.0 to 3.0 hour CLE, plus optional ethics credit. It clearly outlines a step-by-step plan of action to manage a law practice online and build a strong and ethical web presence. The program includes ethical strategies for websites and emailing as well as the simple techniques that will help attorneys avoid several major pitfalls.

Attorneys Will Learn:

Focus Area #1: Optimize Your Website: *Ethically and Properly*

Focus Area #2: Local Listing Directories and Google Places: *Issues Surrounding Reviews and Optimization*

Focus Area #3: Blogging: *What You Can and Can't Do, Including Client Confidentiality & Disclaimer Violations*

Focus Area #4: Social Media: *How Law Firms Should Social Media and Avoid Costly Ethical Violations*

Unlike similar classes, this educational CLE delivers the real substantive content that law firms need to navigate their online presence. Upon completing the CLE, attorneys will understand the best practices for ethically using the Internet and also how to avoid the traps of self-reviewing, improperly commenting on their blog, or misrepresenting their services online.

Reputation Defense for Attorneys: *Ethics and/or General Credit (NEW)*

Attorneys are faced with a difficult challenge in today's digital age: How do you manage your online reputation? With social media, Google, and mobile search being used to research law firms, attorneys must now defend both their offline and online reputation.

This 60 minute, 90 minute, or 1/2 day presentation qualifies in most states for 1.0 to 3.0 hour CLE, plus optional ethics credit. By the end of this CLE, attorneys will know how to find what is being said about them online as well as what steps they can ethically take to control their online reputation. They will discover what assets they need to have online, while also learning how to avoid costly mistakes that can get any law firm in serious trouble.

Attorneys Will Learn:

Focus Area #1: The Myths About Your Online Reputation

Focus Area #2: The 10 Steps You Can Take to Control Your Online Reputation

Focus Area #3: The Ethics of Being Online and Participating in Social Media

Focus Area #4: Simple Steps Every Law Firm Can Take to Monitor Their Reputation Online

Unlike similar classes, this educational CLE delivers the real substantive content that law firms need to navigate their online presence. Once the CLE is complete, attorneys will understand the best practices for ethically using the internet as well as how to avoid the traps of self-reviewing, improperly commenting on their blog, or misrepresenting their services online.

The Ethics of Being Online for Attorneys – Ethics credit only

Every attorney knows they need an online presence. What they also need to know are the ethical ramifications of establishing an online presence as a licensed attorney. Learning how to properly and ethically navigate their online presence is crucial for attorneys as they move into this digital age.

This 60, 90 or 120-minute presentation qualifies in most states for 1.0 to 2.0 Ethics CLE credit. It clearly outlines a step-by-step plan of action to ethically manage a law practice online and build a strong web presence. The program includes ethical strategies for websites and emailing, as well as simple techniques that will help attorneys avoid major online ethics violations. From disclaimers to social media, attorneys will learn the best approach to establishing a web presence without violating any ethical standards.

Attorneys will Learn:

Focus Area #1: Ethically and Properly Establishing Your Web Presence

Focus Area #2: Ethical Issues Surrounding Reviews and Optimization

Focus Area #3: Blogging: What You Can and Can't Do Including Client Confidentiality & Disclaimer Violations

Focus Area #4: Social Media Blunders and How to Avoid Them

Unlike many other similar classes, this educational CLE delivers substantive, useful content that law firms need to navigate their presence online. Upon completion of the CLE, attorneys will understand the best practices for ethically using the Internet and also how to avoid ethics traps like self-reviewing, improperly commenting on their blog, or misrepresenting their services online.

"As you can see from the enclosed evaluations, the attendees thoroughly enjoyed your presentation. One of the attendees said "These guys are great, every attorney should attend this." Another attorney said, "They really know their stuff. I could have sat through an entire day learning and listening from them." Again, thank you for everything you did to ensure a successful seminar." **Jeannie Motylewski Executive Director Lorain County Bar Association**

2012 and Early 2013 CLE Book Tour

We were excited to kick off our CLE Book Tour after the release of our Amazon #1 Best Selling Law Office Marketing Book – *How to Turn Clicks Into Clients*.

This educational CLE course received rave reviews in 2012. Combined with the launch of our revised book *Online Law Practice Strategies*, we have been invited to provide our CLE course by bar associations across the country. As part of our 2013 and 2014 book tour we will be waiving our speaking fee at select events.

Here are some places we delivered CLE's in 2012 and early 2013:

Bar Associations and Events

Sonoma County, CA	Centra, PA
Santa Barbara, CA	Dayton, OH
Memphis, TN	Indiana State Bar Annual
Atlanta, GA	Knoxville, TN
Alameda, CA	Topeka, KS
Oakland, CA	Stark County, OH
Palo Alto, CA	Fairfield, OH
Chicago, IL	Cleveland, OH
Maricopa, AZ	Akron, OH
Nashville, TN	Toledo, OH
Sacramento, CA	Weld County, CO
Chattanooga, TN	Perrysburg, OH
Oakland, CA	Virgina Beach, VA
Louisville, KY	Winter Bar, DC (Bench to Bar)
San Diego, CA	Legal Marketing
Riverside, CA	Association, Las Vegas
Pensacola, FL (Bench to Bar)	Warren County, OH
New Orleans, LA (State Bar)	Colorado State Bar
Columbus, OH (State Bar)	Association
Chattanooga, TN	Chester County, PA
Louisville, KY	Alaska State Bar Association
Butler County, OH	Boston, MA

GLOSSARY

ANALYTICS

Analytics are technical measure you can take to see what happens with visitors on your website: how long they stay, what they click, how many of them return to the website, and statistics of that nature. One of the best analytic software packages out there currently is Google Analytics, which is also free.

AUTORESPONDER

An autoresponder is a system put in place to automatically respond to communication initiated by a potential client, usually via email. Autoresponders can range from simple to extremely complex, and can either send just one generic email or choose from dozens of templates depending on the form used by the potential client or the information provided to the autoresponder by the potential client.

BING

A major search engine, like Google and Yahoo. It has many of the same features and has the next-largest market share of any of the search engines, after Google.

BLOG

Originally an abbreviation of the term "web log", it has now come to mean a type of website (or part of a website) that is frequently updated with new content and has many interactive options for users to leave comments and otherwise participate; many blogs are powered by software explicitly designed to make this frequent updating an easier and smoother process, like Wordpress or Typepad.

CALL TO ACTION

Content on a website or other method of communication that appeals to the reader to contact the business.

CRM

An acronym for "Customer Relationship Management". In the context of internet marketing, it most often refers to the software put in place that manages clients and potential clients of the firm; names, locations, likes, dislikes, needs, and other information that the firm may find relevant.

DIRECTORY LISTINGS

In the sense of Internet marketing, a website or part of a website whose purpose is to list businesses. Many of these, like Yelp, merchant circle, or citysearch, also contain reviews of businesses that are often user-generated and submitted.

DUPLICATE CONTENT

Identical content that appears on multiple websites. Search engines have created ways of detecting this and often have algorithms that even detect if the content has just been altered slightly; content that has just be altered slightly and is still virtually identical to the original content will still be flagged as duplicate content by many search engines.

E-COMMERCE

The buying and selling of products and services over the Internet.

FACEBOOK

A social networking site that is currently the most popular in the world; it allows users to network with each other and socialize, including sharing photos, thoughts, status updates, and wall posts with each other.

FACEBOOK PLACES

A specific segment of the social networking site Facebook that allows users to see local spots around them as well as update their location in real-time from mobile phones or other means, allowing other users to see where they are at any given time.

GEO-LOCATION

In internet marketing and SEO, a term used to describe location-specific information; normally city and state for most local businesses.

GOOGLE MAPS

A part of Google's website that primarily deals with maps and navigation. One of the features of Google Maps is the ability for local businesses to list themselves on it, and the local search return feature was originally a part of this system; Google later integrated it into the main search system when it proved to be popular.

GOOGLE+ LOCAL (Formerly Google Plus)

A part of Google's website that allows a business to have a specific page dedicated to them. It often hooks in with their location on Google Maps, and it features user-generated reviews of the business as well as links to other directories and review sites.

IP ADDRESS

A unique number that identifies a computer on a network.

KEYWORD

A term that a user searches against in a search engine to retrieve content that contains or is relevant to the term.

KEYWORD DENSITY

The use of a specific keyword present in any given piece of content. For example, given the keyword "racing" used five times in a 500 word blog post, the keyword density of "racing" would be 1%. Optimal keyword density is between 3 and 4%, and should not exceed 4% or it may be flagged as spamming.

KEYWORD PHRASE / LONG TAIL KEYWORD PHRASE

A phrase comprised of individual words but treated like a single keyword for the purposes of a search, like "Nascar car racing" or "racing opportunities in Texas".

KEYWORD RICH

Content that has many keywords and uses them often, with good keyword density.

KEYWORD STUFFING

Adding as many keyword(s) in the copy on a website as possible. This technique is very harmful for both search results and website conversion rates.

KEYWORD TOOL

Tools created to help select optimal keywords for search engine marketing, like Google's Keyword Tool. They often contain information such as amount of searches for a particular keyword and other metrics that help ascertain how popular or prevalent a given keyword or keyword phrase may be.

LINKEDIN

A social networking site that is geared towards businesses and professionals, enabling them to link up and network more effectively.

LOCAL SEARCH RETURN

A feature within Google's search engine that returns location-specific results for a user who types in keywords that relate to local businesses. For example, a local search return would appear for a user in Omaha, Nebraska who typed in "law firm elder law"; a map and local businesses that are relevant to the search result would appear in the ensuing search page.

MOBILE WEBSITE

A website that is specifically designed for viewing on a mobile device. This website is separate from your desktop website. Search engines rank mobile websites differently than desktop websites and thus a mobile site must be optimized for mobile search.

MOBILE SEARCH

The term used to describe a search engine on a mobile device.

NICHING

The practice of specializing your marketing strategy to a certain keyword or keyword phrase in order to rank in the highest spot in a local search return for that keyword or keyword phrase.

RESPONSIVE WEBSITE

A website that has been designed to change appearance based on the size of the screen ranging from desktops, tablets to mobile phones. This is different from a mobile website and is generally not recommended for best search results.

ROI

An acronym for "Return on Investment", which means the amount of profit; in literal terms, the amount of money returned for the amount of money invested.

SEARCH ALGORITHM

A series of computer algorithms used by major search engines to index, search, and rank websites on the Internet.

SEARCH ENGINE

A website or company, like Google, Bing, or Yahoo, that indexes other websites on the Internet and allows users to enter keywords in order to find relevant websites.

SEO

An acronym for "Search Engine Optimization". It refers to the section of marketing that tries to increase exposure and clientele by using techniques and strategies to rank high on Internet search engines. Often interchanged with SEM (Search Engine Marketing)

SOCIAL MEDIA

Sites whose primary purpose is to enable users to share content with each other and socialize on the Internet; examples of websites that fall into this category are Facebook, Twitter, and LinkedIn.

SPAM

In Internet parlance, spam was originally used to refer to any unsolicited bulk messages sent over email. It is now also commonly used to refer to content on the Internet which is not useful and designed to make a page rank higher on search engines by tricking search engine algorithms into rating the content as more useful than it actually is.

TWEET

An individual post on Twitter.

TWITTER

A social networking service that allows users to post 140-character tweets to their account, with the ability for other users to follow them and respond to the tweets.

UNIQUE SELLING POSITION

What separates your product, services or offering from your competitors. Something that is unique to you or your firm. Used primarily in marketing to create separation from competitors or establish worth to prospects.

URL

An acronym for "Uniform Resource Locator". It is the name that the user types into the browser bar in order to access a specific website; for example, "www.google.com" or "www.bing.com" would be examples of URLs.

Resources from Previous Chapters:

Keyword Tool Resources

www.GetNoticedGetFound.com/keywordresources

Sample Blog Resources

http://www.GetNoticedGetFound.com/sampleblogs

Press Release Resources

www.GetNoticedGetFound.com/pressreleases

Video Resources

www.GetNoticedGetFound.com/samplevideo

Social Media Resources

http://www.GetNoticedGetFound.com/blog

Directory Listing Resources

www.GetNoticedGetFound.com/directories

Getting Reviews Resources

www.GetNoticedGetFound.com/reviewwhitepaper

Changes in Mobile Resources

http://www.GetNoticedGetFound.com/mobile

Thank You!

Get Noticed Get Found Inc.

7577 Central Parke Blvd. Ste.204

Mason, OH 45040

513.444.2016

or email

Expert@GetNoticedGetFound.com